HOW TO TRAIN YOUR POLITICIAN

Intentional Voting As a Path to Tea Party
& Constitutional Victory

By Ed Hanks

Speechwriter ● Press Secretary ● Political
Consultant

HOW TO TRAIN YOUR POLITICIAN

Copyright 2014 by Ed Hanks and Ten South LLC

Aurora, Colorado, USA

ISBN-13: 978-1500490850
ISBN-10: 1500490857

First Edition: Oct 2014

Cover Design by Ed Hanks

Dedicated to my wife, Lolita, who I met at a
Young Republicans meeting. She was so
passionate about trying to volunteer
her precious time for political causes,
I just had to get to know her.
The rest is history.

Acknowledgments

I'm sure my wife Lolita thinks, "Oh no!" every time I undertake a new writing project on the side. Writing books is so disruptive to "family time," so I deeply value her patience and encouragement. She's also always been a step ahead of me, politically, and I appreciate the intellectual challenges she presents me with.

Thank you, Dad, for teaching me reason, patience and balance. Thank you, Mom, for teaching and guiding and encouraging me, and for demonstrating for me the importance of political passion and involvement.

There are many people – far too many to name individually – who were additionally responsible for getting me into politics and teaching me valuable lessons along the way. To name a few, Pastor Bob Dugan, who ran for Congress when I was five and provided my first political experience. Edie Bryan and Fmr. Rep. Jim Moore for encouraging me to get into politics "for real." Governor Bill Owens – I deeply appreciate the opportunities and education you provided to a young staffer, and I hope you will forgive me for using you as an example, not always in flattering ways. Steve Vieregg, my partner and mentor in the House press office, from whom I learned an astonishing amount about politics and public communications. Speaker Doug Dean and Chief Clerk J.R. Rodrigue for the opportunity to serve with you and Steve, and the wise and hard working Fmr. Reps. Vickie Agler and Joe Stengel for being so great to brainstorm with. Also to all the inspirational political figures over the years who've stuck to their guns and principles.

I must credit Pastor Bob Enyart for many of the concepts discussed in this book. Many of the topics here have been explored on his radio show, or in talks he's given. But also, he is personally responsible for bringing me and my wife into the pro-life movement, and his teachings on Biblical discernment have informed much of what is written here. He challenged many of my old Establishment assumptions and sometimes dragged me away from them kicking and screaming.

I also value the unique group of people Bob and others have raised up to fight for Personhood. Leslie Hanks (only related philosophically), Susan and the rest of the Sutherland clan, Keith and Jennifer Mason, Cal Zastrow and his amazing family, Ken and Jo Scott, Jason and Rachel Troyer, Brian Rohrbough, Josh Craddock and family, Gualberto Garcia Jones, Rosalinda Lozano and many others I know I'm not remembering right now. This group has been like William Wilberforce's inner circle to me. With God's help and these people I have confidence we can overthrow the regime of abortion.

Thank you to all my friends on Facebook who've honed my debating and writing skills, and to those open minded enough to consider the ideas presented here in this book.

Ed Hanks
5 October, 2014

HOW TO TRAIN YOUR POLITICIAN

Intentional Voting As a Path to Tea Party & Constitutional Victory

Don't vote for Squishy!

SQUISHY

by Ed Hanks

Table of Contents

Preface   1

Ch. 1 - Introduction: We Are Being Used   5

Ch. 2 - Things We "Know" That Ain't So   25

Ch. 3 - Compromise Results in Lost Elections   39

Sidebar: Not Voting   52

Ch. 4 - Compromise Results in Bad Government   55

Ch. 5 - Only Nixon Could Go To China   69

Ch. 6 - Intentional Voting   93

Ch. 7 - The Tea Party & Third Parties   99

Ch. 8 - A Plea To Christian Conservatives   115

Ch. 9 - Let's Win Instead of Compromising!   147

Ch. 10 - How To Train Your Politician   185

Afterword   205

Preview: An Introduction to Pro-Life Personhood   207

Preface

I have been an active participant in Colorado politics since I was 5, when I helped my Mom stuff envelopes for a conservative candidate for Congress. I don't know how much *actual* help I provided, but it set up a lifelong interest in politics and government.

At 13 I was making phone calls for Sen. Bill Armstrong's (R-CO) re-election. I participated in my first neighborhood political caucus at 17 (because I would turn 18 on election day this was permitted – Colorado is one of a handful of states that still use a Norman Rockwellesque neighborhood caucus as the first round of candidate and delegate selections, which I still believe is closest to what the Founding Fathers intended as best for a small-R republican government in America). I was helping to run campaigns already as a teenager. Later years would see me hold senior campaign positions, win status as an alternate delegate to the Republican National Convention, and serve as speechwriter to Gov. Bill Owens (R-CO) and press secretary to Republican legislators in the Colorado State House.

Since then I've worked outside of politics, but always maintained a hand. In these recent years I've consulted on various conservative campaigns. I've also exerted a great deal of energy on behalf of the pro-life movement over the past decade, consulting with the Personhood movement in Colorado and assisting with candidate evaluations. I've briefed many officials and candidates for office on pro-life issues.

Despite having a wide range of experience in government and politics, and despite having held more prestigious positions, perhaps the thing that has most qualified me to write this book is serving as Correspondence Director in the Governor's Office. For four years I read virtually every letter that constituents wrote to the Governor. I also saw most every letter of response, and had a hand in crafting many of them.

That job gave me a keen, unique view of what the people of Colorado believe and why. Gov. Owens was popular around the country, so I also got an idea of views in other states. Correspondents would explain their feelings on every issue and lay their thoughts bare. I learned to identify what characteristics led people to believe one thing, as opposed to those which guided another. The rationale behind whole factions of political beliefs became evident. It was an education in personal and bloc politics – both broad and deep – unparalleled outside of that particular job field.

Through comparing arguments in those letters I gradually became more conservative than Owens was, even as he and his staff became less so. It's a lesson which greatly contributed to this book's content.

I originally wrote the material you'll see in this book as part of another book I've been writing about the pro-life Personhood movement, which itself should be published relatively soon. I decided this section was out-of-scope for that volume, but the concepts were so important I decided to turn it into its own project.

The contents of this book are meant to help the conservative movement – tracing its roots through Calvin Coolidge, Barry Goldwater and Ronald Reagan, and reborn again with the Tea Party – understand its value and importance, show where we've been misdirected against our purpose, and to instead lay out a path to new victories against socialism and authoritarianism and restoration of those things Americans have traditionally held dear.

I would invite comments, discussion and constructive criticism at my blog, Look on the Right Side (www. lookontherightside.com). If you convince me I'm wrong about parts of this book I'd be glad to revise my thoughts in subsequent versions.

Don't expect me to roll over easily. In several years of knock and tumble political debate I've heard just about every argument and know how to refute them.

If you like this book, especially if it influences the way you think about things, I would encourage you to please tell others about it, to write a review on Amazon or other book sites, or even to purchase copies to send to pastors, political officials, talk show hosts, bloggers, etc.

So much change needs to occur, and it's not going to happen if we keep quiet about it!

Please also share links to this book's Amazon page on social media, please "like" my author page on Facebook (Facebook.com/conservativechange), follow me on Twitter (@ReagansLegacy), and sign up for my e-newsletter through my Blog, at LookOnTheRightSide.com.

Chapter 1
Introduction:
We Are Being Used

Ideally, political parties are formed around a core set of beliefs and values, ideas and concepts.

It would seem natural, then, for the leaders of that party to work to further those ideals and want to enact policies to implement consistent solutions.

You would think an ideas-based party would be able to accomplish great things, like the Republican Party ending slavery, or the Democrat Party ending poverty.

In fact, millions of Americans *do* think that – do expect great things to happen when they elect members of their party to office.

Every election cycle tens of thousands of volunteer activists work their hearts out during summer and fall and tens of millions of voters flock to the ballot box in November fully expecting that if they can win a big enough victory things will change for the better in America.

Unfortunately, party leaders can grow insensitive to the party's ideas, policies and principles, its very history. They stop listening to its grass roots membership.

They become entirely focused on winning, as if nothing else matters.

Don't get me wrong. Winning is important.

So long as it's for a good purpose, anyway.

There's a quote from the Bible: "What good is it to win the whole world but lose your soul?"

Today's GOP leadership wants to win with a party that has lost its soul.

Without those conservative principles and ideas that make up the Republican platform, what good does it do to control the government?

Democrat activists may even mourn the loss of their own party's ideals. What's President Barack Obama doing, speaking out against the rich, then hob-nobbing with them at bacchanalian fundraisers days later? What's this about trillions of dollars given to bankers in bailouts during, say, the mortgage crisis? What about the people who lost their homes?

Today I think a significant population of realists in both major parties, not to mention many observers outside those parties, are starting to recognize the loss of purpose and principle in the two major parties.

The parties have ceased trying to solve problems and have instead become contributors to the miasmic swamp America is mired in.

I suspect much of this has to do with the "spoils of victory" – the jobs earned for party members, and the perks and handouts leaders and officials are able to get, or give away, to their rich political friends.

This is not upsetting to conservative idealists alone.

Both the Democrat and Republican parties have been infected with a virulent strain of "corporatism" which puts the public treasury at the disposal of a few individuals with the power to buy elections.

Activists on both sides have regarded this trend with growing dismay.

In my own political journeys I have been both a Republican and a moderate-progressive (during high school and college, though I remained a registered Republican). My experiences have convinced me of two things. One, that most progressive voters are sincere and well-meaning in their

6

beliefs and intentions to solve all the problems of the world. Two, that the ideas that make up the Republican platform have the potential to solve most of those same problems, while progressive Democrat ideas never will, nor could they ever, given the mislaid assumptions which underlie them.

I want to be clear that I'm not calling "moderate Republicans" corporatists. I considered myself a moderate at one time, and I know these are sincere people who believe America is best served by staying away from any "extreme" philosophies.

At the same time I do believe moderate Republicans have unwittingly contributed to corporatism because when you take away the strong ideological issues in the GOP platform, all you really have left is improving the economy and "encouraging" business. Many moderate Republicans think business is best supported through government intervention, which is how we got where we are.

In any case, neither party will ever solve America's most fundamental problems without a huge dose of reform.

I grieve that most of the leaders and officials of my own "ideas party" have grown so corrupt and cynical.

As such, reform of the Republican Party and/or victory for the conservative movement are the primary aims of this book.

It is written for the benefit of conservatives, liberty activists, constitutionalists, Tea Party members and Reagan Republicans who want their party back. I also include libertarians and Libertarians as fellow travelers of a sort.

But even many Democrat voters and activists will sympathize with my anti-Establishment message.

How did two "great parties" – the parties of Ronald Reagan, Harry Truman and John F. Kennedy – lose their way?

Take your party back! Reform both, ideally. America benefits not at all by having either major party controlled by a philosophy of corporatism.

Corporatism is a Trap

There's nothing wrong with being rich or building large businesses (which provide jobs the rest of society relies upon).

Certainly, redistributive fiscal policies which take from the rich and give to the poor are not only anathema to capitalism, but they represent theft of property (money) by the state. How much better could it be, then – worse, surely – to take from the middle class, the poor, and even the rich, in order to support certain elites who are favored by the party in power?

Corporatism is a form of socialism exerted on behalf of the rich, instead of the poor.

Redistributive taxation is corrosive to both conservative and capitalist principles.

It is tyranny, no matter who it benefits. It's authoritarianism and control – the hallmarks of leftism.

And corporatism will look out for its own. Freedom and liberty will be curtailed anytime either interferes with the purposes of the state.

If America does not defeat the regime of corporatism and return to principle-based government, our society will increasingly be forced to serve the purposes of the elite.

I do not mean to flog the "corporatist" horse. I consider corporatism to be just another form of statist socialism, manifested through corporate welfare, so hereafter when I refer to "socialism" you'll know I may also mean corporatism.

We have to defeat this ogre before it grows too powerful – while we still have the strength to resist. I credit the Tea Party, and the conservative movement built by Sen. Barry Goldwater (R-AZ) and President Ronald Reagan, with having the potential to do what must be done.

But only if we – the rescuers – do not lose our way.

Reagan's Platform Is Good – Use It!

The ideas – the stated ideals and principles – of the Republican Party are centered around having the liberty to live your life, the freedom to choose where those choices don't harm another individual, respect for the Constitution and the freedoms outlined in the Bill of Rights, and the ability to craft a legacy of financial security for your children through hard work or cleverness.

To be clear, the Republican Party platform emphasizes job growth and "encouraging business" as important for ensuring the future of the country. But philosophically, conservatives have always meant getting government out of the way of business so capitalism works – streamlining unnecessary regulations, reducing taxes to encourage growth, etc.

Conservative philosophy has *never* meant propping up businesses with subsidies, which President Reagan not only opposed, but *mocked*!

He said, "Government's view of the economy could be summed up in a few short phrases. If it moves, tax it. If it keeps moving, regulate it. And if it stops moving, subsidize it."

These conservative ideals are inscribed in the party platform every election cycle. It's clear to read what the grassroots of the party – us – have determined should be the foundational principles the party should stand by.

Conservative stalwarts work to maintain these foundational principles. They band together in groups like the "Republican Assemblies" – a coalition of statewide groups that style themselves "The Republican Wing of the Republican Party." Or 9/12 clubs. Or the Tea Party.

But even as we remain steadfast, much of the party seems to have been demoralized and drawn off into Establishment patterns.

This is *not* a new battle! In Goldwater's 1964 book *Conscience of a Conservative* – 50 years ago – he bemoans the lack of differentiation between the two parties. How Republicans seem only interested in increasing the budget more slowly, rather than reining in government spending and control.

It's clear the party leadership – the Republican Establishment – has its own agenda.

They encourage and spend the Party's vast resources to push nominees who the party membership doesn't want, and who will work to undermine party principles.

The party leadership *should* be beholden to the grass roots. *We elect them!* They should serve us.

But they don't.

The Establishment's Black Box

So, if conservatives have enough power to drive formation of the party platform, which requires a majority at the party conventions and assemblies, you might ask how is it we end up with bad nominees in the first place?

Couldn't we use that same majority to nominate people who believe what *we* believe?

The reason we control one process, and not the other, is twofold.

First, the Republican National Committee and its state party branches have their hands on the levers of power, their thumbs on the scales, and they can use this power to tip the balance. They set many of the rules and also exercise great leeway in the interpretation of other rules set by the grass roots.

Many times, the fix is in before we even get to the table.

At the 2012 Republican National Convention, party leadership and supporters of Mitt Romney conspired to change the rules to give the nominee more control over the process of drafting the party platform – an insidious, incestuous and anti-democratic reversion back to the trappings of the era of "smoke filled rooms."

And party apparatchiks lean on delegates and manipulate the process (which they largely control) to favor their chosen candidate over those candidates preferred by the grass roots. The degree of influence exerted by the rulemakers and talking heads (both within the party structure and in the conservative media, which often takes direction from party leadership) is quite extraordinary.

When the party chairman keeps telling delegates the party is going to lose unless you nominate moderate candidates who won't rock the boat, many of us – the less cynical – are tempted to believe them.

Even otherwise rational conservative delegates can fall into the trap of helping the Establishment, thinking they have to do everything they possibly can to help the nominee. They've been taught it's a sacred duty, even if the nominee's platform is directly at odds with their own beliefs.

Too many conservative activists and delegates have bought into the lie that a conservative "can't win in November – only a moderate can actually win, because conservatives are seen as 'extreme,'" even though these same delegates may hold a hard line on the actual platform issues.

That's one reason.

Secondly, because of all this arsenal of influence exerted by the "powers that be," the conservative candidates who believe in the party's principles have often dropped out by the time of the convention. They've been browbeaten (or gone willingly, thinking they're doing the right thing) into endorsing the anointed candidate, regardless of his principles.

The Establishment has worn them out. And their supporters, too.

Chained to Useless Behaviors

Conservatives, we're shooting ourselves in the foot.

I can't tell you how many times in 2012 I heard someone say their favorite candidate for president was Newt Gingrich, Rick Santorum or Herman Cain, "But they can't win. Only Romney has the moderate views and enough personal money to win," and *"We all have to come together behind him or we'll get Obama again!"*

That plan sure worked, didn't it?!

Romney was (and remains!) plastic and out of touch. His views are too moderate to excite the GOP's conservative base, and not progressive enough to attract voters on the other side or in the middle. His views are inconsistent and have flip-flopped continuously during his long political career (Google "Romney Fairy Tale" for an eye-opening ad that helped defeat him in the 2008 primary, rated the "Best Low-Budget Political Ad" of 2008 by RedState.com).

And Romney's personal fortune probably hurt him more than it helped him. It's okay for Democrats to be multi-millionaires running for office. There are hundreds of them! But if you're a Republican you're a "stinking rich politician trying to buy the election."

President Obama was politically wounded and not at all popular, coming into the 2012 elections. It seemed to many that anyone could have defeated him. Yet Romney couldn't. I predicted that in 2008, in 2011, and again (loudly!) in 2012, but the party (with the aid of many of my conservative friends) nominated him anyway.

We were lied to. We've been trained to do what the Establishment and their talking heads tell us to do. Yes, I'm even looking at some of your favorite conservative television personalities and radio hosts!

Don't feel like I'm accusing you, or calling you less than intelligent. I've fallen victim to these tactics myself, in the past.

I've been lured in before.

I'm not happy about it.

We've all been trained to think the way they want us to. To respond to situations the way they want us to. We've been *trained* to act against our own interests.

How did it happen?

How did *we let it* happen?

A Strategy Driven By Fatalism & Fear

At all levels, from local to presidential politics, the Republican Party hierarchy in the 21st Century has had one foremost operational strategy. It's *not* been to raise a new generation of forward-looking believers who share the conservative philosophy.

Instead, it's been to cultivate and promote candidates who they presume will sound reasonable to the widest variety of *non*-Republican voters, twisting the system to nominate Establishment-friendly candidates who have no interest in reforming the system or implementing conservative principles.

Then they frighten *conservative* voters into voting for these unappealing nominees who've been anointed by party leadership, "or else someone *worse* will win."

All this makes sense... If you agree with the fatalism of the Establishment, which believes no one can win with a conservative philosophy, and that it's better to give up on our principles so we can win.

This is why Republican leadership, for years at the national and state level, has been pushing for more "open primaries" which allow Democrats and Independents to help choose the Republican Party nominees.

This tactic was most recently, and most visibly, used in Mississippi's primary for the US Senate, where a conservative candidate was squeezed out by party leadership and suffered defeat in the primary because moderate and Democrat voters chose the moderate Republican over the conservative.

In Mississippi in November, I'd lay odds that the moderate Republican, Thad Cochran, will lose because the majority of non-Republican voters who voted for him in the primary will prefer the Democrat over the Republican, no matter *how* moderate he is.

Besides that, moving to the center is dangerous in the Deep South. He's opened himself to an *en passent* move (chess) by his opponent, who could move to the right and try to make himself look more conservative than Cochran! That's a switchup you could only see if Republicans have wandered from their moorings.

Open primaries will be discussed more in Chapter 3. They were a primary reason for progressive John McCain's victory in the 2008 primaries, and were a factor in Mitt Romney's 2012 nomination.

The concept of open primaries seems logical on the surface, but is a deeply flawed idea.

The second choice of most — the least offensive choice to the broader population — is not *necessarily* the first choice of any, and in a contest against someone who *is* the first choice of many, they'll lose every time.

It's a self-defeating strategy, but GOP leadership insists on following it because open primaries provide the results they want. More on that later.

Parties Train Voters

The Party assumes (wrongly) no one has the ability to attract independent and moderate voters to support conservative candidates.

They could spend their time educating moderate and independent voters on how conservative views will work, or how progressive Democrat policies are bad.

Instead, they discourage openly conservative candidates, encourage moderates, and seek to train their own voters to settle for what they don't want.

They're just not willing to do the hard work to understand and spread the conservative message.

Consistently, the behavior of party leadership has been to instill fear in their own base – to coerce them into making choices they do not want – *not* to give them confidence and to provide sincere and valuable support for a candidate the people (*our* people) chose!

They want likely GOP voters to think disaster will befall them if they don't vote for all Republican candidates, no matter whether these candidates promise to uphold party values or instead mean to subvert them.

It goes way beyond "get out the vote" – it's full blown intimidation and manipulation.

The Republican candidate is sold as "the lesser of two evils" – they are presented as more conservative and less scary by degrees than their Democrat Party alternative, no matter how moderate or socialistic their politics might be.

The GOP Establishment can and does play this card every election, but it has worked less effectively in every cycle since 2008 due to activists' growing dissatisfaction with the party Establishment.

Gradually, we're catching on.

The Tea Party movement is the most visible evidence of that dissatisfaction, and poses the most formidable obstacle to the success of the Establishment.

But many conservatives aren't quite sure what to do – we resent the manipulation, but still resonate with the conviction that "anyone" is better than a Demcrat.

Conservatives get steamed and grumble about how bad the GOP nominees are these days. But most don't realize they've been enlisted, their behavior craftily twisted.

15

They have not yet fully realized that our own behavior *contributes* to this growing problem.

The practical result of the Establishment strategy is a frustrated and increasingly angry base, on the one hand, and a massive number of Republican politicians on the other who adhere to party principles only slightly, if at all, or who pay only lip service and commit a minimum of effort to legislation which mimics what is demanded by the grass roots.

Some of the most historic socialistic policies have been perpetrated by Republican congressmen, Republican governors and Republican presidents in recent years. Medicare D? Romneycare? Bailouts of private corporations to the tune of trillions of taxpayer dollars?

These are not conservative values. These are not even capitalist principles. These acts represent socialism at work, pushed by Republican politicians and officials at the behest of the Establishment.

The Establishment is most focused on "jobs and the economy." That, by itself, is perfectly responsible.

But they're not pursuing their goal through capitalist or conservative pro-business means, by "getting government out of the way." Mostly they want to provide government support for private enterprise – *certain* private enterprises – who are their friends.

That blurs the line between the business sector and government.

This is "picking winners and losers."

It's collusion.

No matter how you try to paint it, it's a perversion of capitalism. It's corporate welfare.

And it's pushed upon the American people by our Republican Party and the Republican officeholders *we've* been voting for!

Raiding the Public Treasury

Again, it's not just Republicans doing this. Both parties' politicians do this. Sometimes favoring different companies. Often, they back the *same* large corporations.

Some huge industry leaders divide their donations to please both parties to cover all bases. Often they give a 60/40 split – barely favoring one party, but keeping both "on the take."

Progressive voters assume "large corporations" back only Republicans, but in reality almost as many are "Democrat corporations," like Microsoft or MCI Worldcom (to name one from the past).

Both parties backed massive bailouts of private corporations without any appreciable framework of accountability for the taxpayers. They just threw money at huge companies (different ones, depending on which party directed the funds) and let them do as they would.

What oversight there was for these hefty government checks showed massive degrees of fraud. Billions of dollars disappeared with no visible benefit to the economy. The heads of several failing companies got million dollar "bonuses," along with their top staffs.

For what? For backing the right party at the horserace, I suppose.

It's a circular process. Corporations back politicians who fund them in return. It's back and forth. You scratch my back, I'll scratch yours.

The system, then, perpetuates itself. Pay to play. On both sides – political and corporate.

It blurs the divide even further, between private sector and government sector, by allowing great corporations influence in government, which itself becomes even more beholden to big industry.

Again, that's *not* capitalism. That's a perversion.

It's not harmless. It's not business as usual.

It's one of the worst forms of corruption.

It's *evil,* because it hurts the country and its people.

Is Obamacare a Government Subsidy to Business?

Obamacare certainly isn't a very effective benefit to *citizens.*

Not that *any* large government programs are likely to be effective in that respect.

So who is it meant to help?

The only two parts of Obamacare which really worked as intended were 1) it hands a huge portion of every American's life and finances over to the government (you thought the *IRS* was intrusive and heavy handed?), and 2) it greatly benefits large insurance companies who get to lessen coverage while charging more for it.

Such a deal!

Now, what do Establishment Republicans intend to do about Obamacare?

Many say they'll "repeal" it. But at times you get the impression that's just election year fluff, meant for the ears of the Tea Party and grassroots Republicans, because it's what we want to hear.

Meanwhile, we *want* to believe them, which is why it works.

But do they really mean repeal? No – most simply intend to modify it. Likely so it will be more like Romneycare, which was just a lesser version of Obamacare.

Less socialistic, less coercive, less controlling, but definitely each of those to a somewhat lesser degree. It's nature is the same as Obamacare.

The Establishment candidates are selling Romneycare as the lesser of two evils.

Or they will. They did, in 2012, to promote Romney's candidacy.

And the Establishment will try again in 2016 if he's a major contender for the nomination.

Other Major Issues

What about all those other issues Republicans talk about? They *can't* be focused only on corporations if we hear about so many other issues. *Can* they?

What about liberty issues? What about social issues?

The greatest irony is that the public, along with most Republican and Democrat activists, really believes the Republican Party is *defined* by its pro-life stands, protection of gun rights, and the rest of this stuff, for better or worse.

"Republicans are *obsessed* with guns & abortion & gays! And birth certificates! No wonder they're losing elections!"

In practice, that's completely untrue. Those things are very far from most Republican candidates' focus. These things are part of the Establishment's plan of manipulation, though.

If the candidates talk right, and we want to be fooled, they never have to actually do anything except mouth the correct words in closed-door speeches and private solicitations for fundraising.

Abortion is a back-burner issue for the Establishment of the party. And gun rights are a place where the Establishment concentrates only because they know they have to (i.e. the gun rights activists have been more effective in controlling the attention of the Establishment than have the pro-life activists).

The Establishment is not interested in protecting rights — not for of citizens of any age or status. They're interested in money, just like the Democrats.

Again, I'm talking about leadership, not moderate or Establishment voters or activists.

The American Dream and the conservative principles that made this country great – liberty, freedom, the right to live your life and build security for your family – they're set by the wayside.

Today's GOP party leadership isn't interested.

Who Should Train Who?

Parties try to train us to do what they want. Perversely, the Republican Establishment has trained us to help them subvert Republican principles.

Many of us have fallen into that trap.

But we don't have to do as we're told. We don't have to respond to fear-based tactics. We are still able to use our own vote in our own interests, not those of the Establishment.

And we are free to take the initiative. *If* we have the courage to do so.

The good news is that political parties and political candidates can be trained too.

We can turn the tables.

Political parties' behavior is learned at every election. They learn – not always quickly – what they did wrong and how to fix it.

Your behavior, as a voter, trains them at every election.

But for them to learn, we have to show them what they did wrong.

Our track record of doing that is poor. Our quality control has been lacking.

The bad news is that we – as Christian conservatives, Tea Party and liberty activists (most of us) – have been teaching Republican Party leadership...

Well...

For the past two decades we've been training the GOP to take us and our votes for granted.

Our habitual behavior has had the unintended consequence of encouraging *their* bad behavior.

We've been *contributing* to the very situation we complain about!

Until recent election cycles I was trapped in that same cycle.

Hope, hold your nose, vote, be disappointed, promise to fight harder next time to make sure we have a conservative nominee...

Then repeat...

It's An Addiction

Gradually, Tea Party Republicans who believe in the party platform are beginning to wake up, but most of us aren't quite sure what we can do.

We know we're trapped, but there seems to be no way out.

We've not made the progress we could have, or need to make.

GOP leadership still knows that most of us will always vote for the "lesser of two evils."

They know we will support the nominee because we've been taught to think the alternative is always worse. They know we believe votes for third parties are "wasted votes" because we think they can't win, and without winning they have no influence.

The Republican Party has trained us expertly. They have confidence that, by November, we'll vote for whoever the party's nominee is. We're creatures of habit.

They've made us "single issue voters" – we'll vote for anyone with an "R" after their name on the ballot. Even if he's got a decades-long record of opposing conservative positions (McCain, Romney)!

Despite our frustration with bad choices every election cycle, they know we are *compelled* to vote for the lesser of two evils because they've trained us to believe there's no way out of our dilemma.

Just so long as they dress him up like a conservative, throw a Ronald Reagan mask on him, and make him say the right things, we'll hold our noses and pull the lever.

And, because of this, they know they're free to ignore us and our views and we'll still vote for their nominee.

This happens at the federal level, and the state legislative level.

Enough!

It's *got* to stop! This vicious cycle is destroying the conservative movement.

What can we do?

Let's stop training them to ignore us!

In 1964 conservatives had gotten angry enough that they "shoved" the political system.

We didn't win the presidency that year, with Sen. Barry Goldwater (R-AZ), but it did start a growing and increasingly vocal movement that twelve years later came within a hair's breadth of toppling a sitting Establishment president in a primary, and which *did* succeed just four years after that by placing conservative Fmr. Gov. Ronald Reagan (R-CA) in the Oval Office.

22

Don't worry. It's not going to take us 16 years to get our party back. We're already almost there.

But to make it happen we have to embrace the concept of "intentional voting" – voting for effect.

And we have to start now.

In this book I will further illustrate how the Establishment's manipulations and heavy-handed tactics have suborned us – activists and voters – in such a way that conservatives keep re-electing these moderate leaders, even when we don't agree with them, both into party positions and into government office.

Then I'll explain how to reverse the process. To teach them they work for us.

Let's train *them* to do what *we* want!

Chapter 2
Things We "Know" That Ain't So

So what methods does the Establishment (GOP and Democrat alike, in many cases) use to train voters to think and act as they want us to?

We know we're being manipulated, but how are they doing it?

Mostly it's done through the spreading of untrue maxims and ways of thinking through "local culture" (i.e. within the party membership), as well as in society as a whole.

And it's not just the Establishment teaching these things. They've taught us to "police ourselves," so when one of us gets rebellious or steps out of line one of our friends takes a point out of this chapter and repeats it to us, all the while thinking they're doing good and speaking truth.

As some wit once said, "It ain't what you don't know that gets you into trouble. It's what you know for sure that just ain't so." The saying has been variously attributed to Mark Twain, Josh Billings and Will Rogers, which is an amusingly ironic illustration of the point.

What are some of these things we *know for sure* "that just ain't so?"

1. We Must Choose The Lesser of Two Evils

Don't we *have* to choose the guy who lied to us about what he believed, and who votes with the Democrats a third of the time, but who agrees with us more than half the time?

Otherwise we get the guy or girl who *always* votes with the Democrats and makes us steaming red in the face on a weekly basis.

Choosing between imperfect candidates is the American way of life! Isn't it?

Don't we face this choice every election? Get used to it.

Besides, "the lesser of two evils" is just a saying, right?

Sometimes it *is* just a saying.

Often, we're choosing between two relatively qualified candidates who simply have different opinions about how to make the country better. We'll agree with one more than the other.

Other times – more frequently than we'd like to admit – we're choosing between two *relatively* corrupt candidates. Let's get the lesser crook!

On some level it makes sense to pick the guy or girl who will do the least damage.

But how far can you take this kind of "damage reduction" thinking?

Damage reduction is surely not the way to reverse any of the bad things we see. Is it even a step in the right direction to reversing them?

Is it really your *duty* as a responsible citizen to choose between the lesser of two evils, no matter what the choices?

Any behavior advised as "always correct" – and we regularly hear talk show hosts and political leaders telling us this is how it is – should stand up in all situations, right?

It's not an absurd suggestion. It's advertised as without practical limits – the behavior you should *always* choose – so it's reasonable to test the maxim against historical situations.

In the 1800s American Christians often faced a choice between two pro-slavery candidates. Sometimes they disagreed about the degree of slavery that should be allowed. Other times they differed not at all on the issue.

When faced with two pro-slavery candidates, how do you choose the lesser evil? Doesn't mere association with the institution of human bondage make it hard to choose a lesser? By choosing the lesser of two evils, Christians (or anyone) were still voting for someone who supported keeping men and women in chains.

In the 1930s German democracy was increasingly challenged by leftist philosophies. Not from left and right, as many historians falsely claim, but rather from a variety of parties ranging from the far left Communists to the socialist "lesser left" Nazis (National Socialists).

In 1932 and 1933 there were three major parties – the Nazis, the Communists and the Socialists – to choose from. Each of these three parties was socialistic, anti-democratic, and authoritarian in nature.

These parties had gangs of thugs roaming the streets at night, attacking opposing gangs and supporters of the other parties. Both the Socialists and Communists were philosophical associates of the Bolsheviks who had murdered 9 million people as a result of their revolution and civil war in Russia. Socialists were seen as Godless supporters of disorder and revolution. Because of this, they seemed to many Germans to be the "worst evil."

There were three smaller parties, of a size like America's third parties today, which were reasonably supportive of western democratic principles. These included the Zentrum (the Catholic Center Party).

Six parties. But by "lesser of two evils" thinking you *must* choose between the most viable two, right? Otherwise you strengthen the *worst* evil, so the theory goes.

What should a person of conscience do, if forced to choose between Hitler and Stalin? Nazism vs. Communism? Each choice supported socialism (sound like an echo of Establishment Republicanism?).

Sadly, in 1932 and 1933 most Christians and otherwise moral people chose Hitler as the "lesser of two evils." He was seen as a protector of traditional morals, and falsely played on Christian themes, whereas Communism was totally opposed to Christianity.

The Germans feared one violent socialistic party less than the others, and voted for what they thought was the lesser of two evils. Many German Christians were afraid of the "boogyman" represented by the socialists and communists. They felt "forced" to vote for who they thought was the man who would save them.

Clearly, choosing the "lesser of two evils" in 1930s Germany had catastrophic results. It was a bad choice.

It was bad advice!

Today our choices are less extreme, but we must make similar comparisons between bad, worse and worst choices.

What if, in 2012, Hillary Clinton had switched parties and became the Republican nominee against Obama? What then?

"Where are the Hillary banners? We've got to run out there and get this girl elected! Otherwise *all is lost!!!*"

What if it were Obama vs. Hitler? Who would be the lesser of two evils we're supposed to support?

Obviously, the "lesser of two evils" mantra is false *in at least some cases*. It's not always the preferred behavior. Or else you'd end up supporting Hitler, maybe. Or at least Obama. Or Hillary.

It makes you wonder if it's *ever* the correct behavior, doesn't it?

I *hope* it makes you wonder!

So when does a candidate go from a necessary, clever, if not optimal, political choice to being an evil choice?

Where do they cross the line?

By voting for the "lesser of two evils" – knowingly accepting faults you've identified as better than the faults of his/her opponent – you are endorsing whatever moral compromises that candidate proposes.

In a flurry of German federal elections in 1932 and 1933 about 22 percent of Germans chose to vote for one of the three smaller, "third parties" instead of for the larger leftist parties.

Did they "waste their votes?" Or did they cast a principled vote, which separated them from responsibility for the evils perpetrated by Hitler, or which might have been perpetrated by the Communists?

Voters cannot be held responsible for unexpected compromises and evils of a candidate or party, but I assert they hold partial responsibility for the decisions made by even "lesser of two evils" candidates whose support of some evil is known beforehand.

Hitler stood against most of what Christians believe, and that was clear to those with open eyes and minds even before his election.

Establishment thinkers will claim those who didn't support the lesser of two evils became "responsible" for Hitler's victory, by not choosing a lesser evil.

I contend that the moral choice would have been to reject each radical philosophy or party. Even if one antithetical philosophy or another is certain to prevail, at least it will happen without your collusion and support.

Without your *endorsement*.

2. We Can't Let the Perfect be the Enemy of the Good

When we try to hold fast to principle, the Establishment – and those who've been trained by the Establishment – remind us of this over and over...

"Don't let the perfect be the enemy of the good!"

It's the phrase they've learned to repeat. It's the phrase they've trained *us* to repeat to each other, when any of us get out of line.

Honestly, who's talking about *perfect* candidates?!

No one I know.

None of our political heroes were or are perfect.

But there are issues where you can give a little, and there are other issues where compromise spells disaster.

Where to chop away at the Bill of Rights, for instance, without ruining its undergirding?

"Why let the perfect be the enemy of the good?"

Hmm…

So are we really holding out for "perfect" or "ideal" candidates? Or are we simply asking for candidates who will stand up for something?

Often, we're just looking for a candidate who will abide by the specifics of the GOP party platform, which is pretty specific but is simple at the same time.

Lower taxes, less spending, fiscal responsibility, less government interference in business and peoples' lives, support for liberty as carefully spelled out by the Founders in the Bill of Rights – those things which enable us to remain a free country.

And if someone held to all but one of those standards, most of us would give them some grace.

The problem is someone who compromises on more than one of those is usually going to compromise on the others too.

I call this using *"gateway standards."* I can give on a lot of things, but not on certain foundational issues.

A candidate doesn't have to be "perfect." But they need to meet the standards I hold as "non-negotiable," otherwise they don't get past my "gateway" for consideration.

What's so extreme about expecting Republican candidates to believe the same as a significant majority of the party? And what's so outrageous about expecting them to do as they promised, once elected?

These two issues are, unfortunately, a major problem with the candidates we've been seeing at the head of the GOP these days.

The Establishment has been pushing these people, because the Establishment – our party leadership! – doesn't care about the tenets of the party platform.

They're failing our most reasonable expectations. It's time for us to stand up. Not for "perfect" party leaders or "perfect" candidates.

Just loyal ones!

3. Moving the Ball Forward

Those who fall into the trap of voting for "lesser of two evils" candidates rationalize to themselves that they're "moving the ball forward," even if they didn't get everything they wanted.

Making progress toward the goal, even if they didn't get a touchdown.

We've been trained to think this way. To think that if we elect someone from the same party – someone we agree with 70 or maybe even just 60 percent of the time – that we've made progress.

It's human nature to want to think we've accomplished some good, even when in the back of our minds we're pretty sure we just had to do something distasteful.

But, as I will show in more detail later on, it's often likely that voting for the lesser of two evils accomplishes more harm than good for our side, and our views.

Don't assume that just because someone stands closer to us "on the political spectrum" they're going to be better for our views and issues than someone who is completely opposed to us.

I used to write strategy guides for computer strategy games, so game strategy is something I understand, as well as its relationship with politics.

It's just a different game when an office is held by someone who believes everything we don't, and vice versa – a game played by different rules, but which may be easier to win than the game we've been playing.

I'll go into this in finer detail later in this book. Please be patient, even if you greatly doubt me, and allow me to make the case.

4. Any Other Vote is a Wasted Vote

Three things, in the minds of the Establishment and those who they've trained, are "wasted votes."

- A non-vote

- A vote for a primary candidate who "can't win"

- A vote for a third party candidate

I can agree on only one – a non-vote is a missed opportunity to work for change.

Cast a ballot for the candidates and offices you can support, and if there's really no one running for an office who isn't some degree of evil, then leave it as an undervote or write someone in.

With regard to the "can't win" candidates, I wonder what might happen if everybody who really preferred that candidate actually voted for them. They *might* win!

I often hear, "You *have* to vote for the Republican, or the Democrat will win!"

This is often followed with or replaced by the correlational, "A vote for a third party is a vote for the Democrats!"

We're told, therefore, that voting for anybody who "can't win" – casting a "protest vote" – is wasting your vote.

It's strange how, in congressional districts where one party normally gets 70 percent of the vote, voting for the major-party candidate who's guaranteed to lose isn't considered "throwing away your vote." In those districts the Republican realistically "can't win." And yet Republicans will be going door to door and calling at all hours of the night urging everybody to vote for the Republican.

Why? They "can't win!" It's just a protest vote! Why bother?

It's not just because of the "upticket" races, like statewide races or presidential contests. It's also because those 30 percent, or even 10 percent, of the votes become protest votes against the leadership of that district, *and they are valuable for that purpose.*

Protest votes are important. They do matter, because they are instructive to both major parties, and they help determine the future behavior of both.

They *train* the parties!

The closer to 50 percent the protest votes get (or 33% in 3-way races), the more the officials will shift their behavior and tone.

If 70 percent of a district is registered Democrats, and the Democrat candidate earns only 60 percent of the vote, *that gets their attention!*

They think to themselves, "We're doing something wrong – we'd better figure out what it is, or we might slip up and a Republican could take that district in a bad year." Or vice versa, if it's a GOP district.

History is full of examples where Democrats or Republicans won "can't win" districts because there was a major mood swing moving through the public, or because there was a scandal. In 1974 Republicans got slaughtered, even in favorable districts, because of Watergate.

So, occasionally, even "protest" votes due to voter anger or dissatisfaction can decidedly affect elections.

Obviously, if the Republican isn't a "lesser evil," and is very much a Republican, our votes would be best spent there.

But when you think about it you're only really "wasting your vote" when you vote for someone out of desperation who doesn't accurately represent your beliefs and values.

By all means, set minimum standards on "gateway issues" and vote for the most likely candidate to win *who meets those standards.*

But in the absence of a major party candidate who fails to meet minimum standards, send a message of no-confidence by voting for the third party which does.

5. Don't Take That Vote Away From Us!

"Don't take your vote away from 'x.' Don't be selfish! He needs that vote!"

What??! My eyes crossed the first time I heard someone say that.

In the 2012 election I was actually told that if I didn't vote for Romney I was "taking my vote away" from him.

What?!

He never had it!

He never *owned* it in the first place!

His record spoke for itself – he had a clear record as a socialist pro-abort and was only disguising himself to look and sound like a conservative pro-lifer. I wasn't going to vote for him!

I never even considered it, because these ideas I've been explaining in this book have been with me for a number of years.

I practice what I preach.

Who owns my vote? *I do!*

Who owns *your* vote? *You do!*

Don't let anyone tell you that because you're registered as a Republican that someone else – a candidate or a party – *owns* your vote, which is exactly what someone means when they say, "Don't take that vote away from..."

6. If You Don't Vote For "X" You're Voting For "Y"!

I've heard this one too. It's a first cousin of the "we own your vote" argument.

"A vote for a third party is a vote for Al Gore!"

No, actually a vote for a third party is a vote for that third party, and the ideas it represents.

A third party vote does not add to either major party candidate's total votes, so the claim is hyperbole at best.

It's manipulative shaming, at worst.

People making this argument always pull out a calculator and show you how "the Republican would have won if the Libertarian hadn't taken 3,000 votes away from him!" Again, it's the ownership thing.

In 1856 there was a third party called the Republican Party. It was where the most passionate anti-slavery voters went, because they didn't feel "heard" by either major party, or because they couldn't bring themselves to vote for the "lesser slavery supporter."

Surely, since Republicans came from both parties, there were cries of, "If you vote for the Republican, you're voting for the Whig!" Or the opposite – "If you vote for the Republican, you're voting for the Democrat!"

But ultimately the Whigs and Democrats were shown up as fools, because voters increasingly refused to believe the scary rhetoric. Instead they voted *for* what they wanted. And they eventually got it.

In every election candidates add votes to their tallies by *earning* votes.

Votes, as it happens, aren't that easy to earn. It's not a zero sum game. Voters come and go.

But an especially hard working and inspiring candidate or party can earn votes that "weren't there" before, or they can earn votes that might otherwise have gone to third parties.

Third parties earn votes because major party candidates are disappointing or uninspiring, or because they don't grasp a growing desire building within a segment of the population.

It's the fault of the major party candidate for not earning that vote, because he doesn't follow the party platform or he's unprincipled.

You're not just following the crowd – you're voting your conscience. You've cast a moral, informed vote for someone you can believe in, and who shares your values.

Vote for someone who *earned* your vote!

7. Third Parties Can't Win and Aren't Effective

I have a section in Chapter 7 (The Tea Party & Third Parties) which addresses this. It's included here simply to point out this is a myth too, because third parties influence politics all the time. They become a lever by which to modify major party behavior, if nothing else.

8. Holding Their Feet to the Fire

I've sometimes heard conservative Republicans suggest that if a squishy Republican is nominated, and we're "forced" to choose the lesser of two evils, that once we get them elected we'll "hold their feet to the fire" and make sure they vote conservative.

This never works.

Election time is the only time we voters really have control over the politicians. There are a few exceptions, like the recall elections held recently in Colorado that overturned three Democrat state senators.

But for the most part once you have invested your time to elect a squishy Republican they can feel free to ignore you until the next election, when you'll again be expected to back the lesser of two evils for re-election because to do anything else would potentially put a weaker, non-incumbent Republican in nomination and they'd be more likely to lose to a Democrat.

They always figure if they fooled you once, it'll be as easy or easier to fool you twice. And so they're likely to continue to ignore you.

There's no "holding their feet to the fire." If you just elected a squish to the US Senate, squishdom will reign for five years before they have to pretend to be interested in your opinions again.

Chapter 3
Compromise Results In Lost Elections

Our choice, as conservatives, to vote for the lesser of two evils, for fear of something worse, has undermined conservatism and conservative principles.

We are *creating* the monster we abhor.

Make no mistake. There are real leaders and statesmen out there who sincerely mean the best.

But the larger population of *mere politicians* will sink to the lowest level we allow them to get away with, and we've failed to exercise our duty of quality control.

It's easy to get discouraged, and you may be tempted in that direction as I go on about these things in detail.

I don't want you to be downcast about our situation.

I want you to get angry!

I want you to channel that passion into a determination to do something about it.

This chapter and in following chapters I will explain in detail how we learned to compromise, and what the historical "fruits" of our compromise have been. What did we get, for all our efforts to elect the lesser of two evils?

Moderates Can Win! (Or Can They?)

Most of you've heard the term "RINO" – Republicans in Name Only.

For those who might not be familiar, it's a candidate or voter who is a Republican by registration but sure doesn't sound or act like one (i.e. they often deviate from the party platform).

Many RINOs consider it a derogatory and offensive term. They prefer labels like "moderate Republican" or "Rockefeller Republican."

The key to why the "Republicans in Name Only" moniker fits is these Republicans are in the extreme minority – they're the ones who voted "no" on most or all of the issues that were approved by 67-95 percent of Republican activists or delegates to define what the party should stand for (i.e. the party platform).

The Establishment, not to mention "conventional wisdom," would have you believe that the closer to the middle of the political spectrum a candidate is, the more likely they are to win.

In other words they want the party to cater to a minority population which represents only 30 to 5 percent of our own party's membership.

We're told over and over that the future of the party is in the hands of these RINO voters and candidates, because they're closer to the mainstream of society.

But is a political party – a force of people collected to support a set of specific partisan ideas – really supposed to represent the average of citizens' opinions *outside* of the party?

Is that what republican democracy was supposed to mean? That sounds more like actual democracy (aka "mob rule"), where everyone gets to vote on everything and the average opinion becomes policy.

It's true that some states and some districts are progressive enough in character that the "baseline" for Republican principles is skewed – the average Republican there is more likely to support a moderate than a conservative, and the average citizen is more likely to support a progressive than a moderate.

I personally maintain this is a messaging problem – if any population of reasonable people had conservatism properly explained to them I believe they'd latch on and embrace it. But I digress.

According to the Establishment, conservatives are the reason why Democrats have been winning in Washington and many state capitals. Democrats are perceived by the public as moderates, while Republicans keep idiotically undertaking a "war on women and gays."

But a reasonable survey of Republican campaign speeches, ads & mailers paints a picture very different from what the Establishment and media would paint. This "framing" of the election situation as Republicans hating gays and constantly harping on abortion bears no resemblance to reality.

Republican speeches are almost always laser focused on jobs and the economy. During the general election especially.

So you'd think if candidates are following the Establishment's rules for how to run a campaign, they'd be winning. They're following the formula.

But the record in most states is clear – Republican moderates don't have a better record of winning elections than conservatives. They often have a *harder* time.

Besides, the Democrat candidates usually aren't moderates. Some of them are loony lefty extremists, and a lot of *those* candidates win!

But why would a Republican moderate, who's closer to the average voter in the kinds of things he says and makes an issue of, still lose to the Democrat in one election after another? Even when it's a case of a moderate Republican against a loony lefty?

And how do some states elect one moderate senator and another conservative one? By the Establishment model, you'd never see conservatives win in those "moderate" states.

Obviously, the Establishment model of "reality" is wrong.

There's more at work here than just a formula to approach closest to the centerline of public opinion.

A Dearth of Ideas, Contrast & Excitement

There are many reasons why moderate candidates don't do well. Partly it's their inability to excite Republicans about their candidacy.

The Establishment tendency to talk about only half of the Republican platform falls flat with many Republicans, including those who became invested in politics in the first place because of non-economic issues, be that social or liberty related.

Others, who comprise the new segment of Tea Party (Taxed Enough Already) members, *did* become engaged because of economic issues, but by and large they activated because they came to some *very* principled conservative realizations of how government affects them.

Not being able to "speak" to these key conservative principles, which many moderate, Establishment candidates can't, results in a "failure to motivate the base."

And when the top party tickets don't feature good, credible, conservative messages, many conservatives and Christians (since 1980 a large segment of the base of the GOP) don't show up to vote.

Many conservatives fail to engage only unconsciously or subconsciously. They don't *mean* to not vote, but they have an easier time giving in to reasonable excuses for not voting. Life is busy – we've got a lot of things to do. Sometimes it takes an exciting candidate who we really agree with just to get people to set aside their lives to fill out a ballot or show up at the voting booth.

So when the base of the party doesn't show up on election day it's a natural result of the Party failing to motivate us – failing to provide a candidate who presents a clear choice.

Maybe the nominee seems so far to the left that

we cannot stomach voting for them. Maybe they seem fake because they can't explain what they believe or why. For one reason or another, many don't vote.

Many who are disappointed but still want their voice to be heard vote third party instead, to make a statement.

That's a valid choice, and resentment against those voters is inappropriate (remember the "who owns your vote" section?).

Often their vote for a third party, or their non-vote, is like a cry of anguish from someone who wishes they could have voted for the nominee in good conscience.

Now, sometimes I say "we" like all of us in the base of the Republican Party vote as a bloc.

This is true to a degree, but thinking in those terms can be misleading.

Because we've been trained, most conservatives *will* vote for the lesser of two evils. Even most Christians will vote for the lesser of two evils, because they've also been trained to think they're still "moving the ball forward" in moral terms.

But there is a significant and growing faction that will not. We've seen this proved in recent election cycles.

Lessening Enthusiasm

The Republican relationship with their own base was mostly okay during the early years of President George W. Bush's administration.

Starting in 2006 a gulf was increasingly apparent between promises made and actual results. In the previous presidential election the President and Congress had promised fiscal conservatism and action on a federal marriage amendment and anti-abortion measures.

Instead, those two years had produced inaction, besides a hate crimes statute (seemingly aimed at vocal Christians re:

marriage), and a huge, expensive entitlement program called Medicare D.

They promised one thing and did the opposite.

Conservatives were incensed by the bait and switch.

In 2006 massive numbers of Christians and true conservatives failed to even show up to vote.

They lacked motivation.

The Establishment can't train everyone. Many conservatives and Christians did vote for the "lesser of two evils." But many more simply stayed home, and it showed.

In 2008, Republican strategizers sensed they'd done something wrong in 2006. Instead of running moderates on "centrist" platforms, they ran moderates on conservative platforms.

They packaged them up, told them their talking points, issued everyone Ronald Reagan masks, and sent them out to talk Christians into thinking they were serious. This energized the base sufficiently to give John McCain (or Sarah Palin, at least) a strong showing of Christian conservative voters.

But McCain wasn't convincing enough. He had developed a record over many years as a moderate "pro-choice" Republican.

For a decade, one of the base's favorite thought- and laugh-leaders, Rush Limbaugh, had justifiably painted McCain as the next thing to a progressive liberal, and just a hair's breadth from being a Democrat.

Many of Limbaugh's fans couldn't "un-see" the vision of McCain as a Democrat!

And a lot of those voters wouldn't hold their nose. They didn't show up.

Though Sarah Palin energized many Christians, a great number still stayed home.

It was a brilliant example of open primaries choosing the absolute wrong candidate.

The 2010 election was another testbed for conservative revolt. Many Tea Party candidates won the primary elections only to have the Establishment pull the rug out from under them. They lost, not because they were bad candidates (though many lacked "prime-time" polish), but because the Establishment crushed them with rhetoric.

The Establishment had a vested interest in their loss – they felt threatened. Both their jobs and their favored policies were at stake. We'll come back to this later.

In 2012 the economy was sluggish, people were angry about Obamacare, most people could recognize US foreign policy was drifting, record-low numbers of Americans felt President Obama was even "there" for America. Ironically, millions of Blacks – Obama's strongest base – had even come to doubt Obama's sincerity and abilities.

Obama's base was de-energized! While Romney was pulling in thousand-seat political rallies, Obama – a sitting president! – was embarrassed to have only a couple dozen supporters at some of his own events!

Political trackers said Obama was down in more than half of the "leading indicators" for an incumbent. No incumbent president in history had ever won with that many factors trending down.

Romney, or *any* Republican, should have won that race in a walk. What happened?

Reagan Was a True Believer

Compare those recent election results to 1980.

Then, as in 2012, you had an angry, energized populace who knew the country was going downhill and wanted to do something about it.

Again – what happened?!

Why, with conditions so very similar, could Romney not replicate Reagan's landslide victory from 1980?

No one was excited about Romney in 2012.

Think about it – even if you thought your life depended on his victory (some of you *did*!), you didn't really feel Romney represented you and your values. If you turned out to vote, it was out of fear, or because you thought he would at least throw the brakes on America's decline. He was the lesser of two evils.

The difference is failure to motivate the base.

Romney also allowed the media and Democrats to define him and frame the debate.

How?

Because Romney couldn't explain why a conservative Republican (i.e. what he was painted up to be) should be the next president.

Why?

Because he *wasn't* a conservative!

He could read talking points, but he couldn't feel the passion of someone who really believed in them.

Moreover, he couldn't communicate why conservative values should lead us into the next eight years because he didn't believe in those values himself.

He tried hard to sound like a champion for freedom and capitalism. But in the undertones of his speeches, conservatives could detect hints of his statist, free-spending instincts.

He didn't want a conservative president, himself!

Romney wanted to head a big, powerful government that would "fix" America.

That's not a conservative vision. That's progressivism.

McCain had the same problem... And suffered the same result.

Yes, winning means having to attract independents, getting them riled up and ready to vote for you. Winning means convincing moderates to see you as the better choice (even if *they* see you as the lesser evil).

Winning may even require you to peel off votes from the other party – earning Democrat votes.

But if your own party – the people who walk precincts and make phone calls, the people who energetically go to bat for their candidates on social media – if they aren't engaged and excited to see you as the next president (or their next legislator) you're going to see a negative impact on turnout.

Maybe you'll pull it out in a squeaker. Maybe you'll underperform and suffer an unexpected loss.

Either way, without the base – the backbone of your own party – you are much less likely to win.

Open Primaries – Don't Popularity Contests Make Sense?

The Establishment loves to use "open primaries" for candidate selection – primary elections where you don't have to be a registered Republican before you choose to vote in the Republican primary. Democrats and independents are given the opportunity to vote for their "favored" Republican.

This concept makes sense on the surface. The idea is that all the state's voters will ultimately make the decision in November, so in the primary you allow as broad a cross-section as possible of the overall voter pool to make the decision, expecting the chosen candidate will be more appealing in the general election than someone who is ideologically skewed to only half the state's (or district's) voters.

It produces a candidate, in the language of the Establishment snobs, not so beholden to the "special interests" of conservative activists.

Note to the Media and Establishment: We're not "special interests." We're the good people of the United States of America who have chosen to participate in the political process and make our views known, as was intended by our Forefathers!

In any case, the idea is flawed on two levels.

One is the "jack of all trades, master of none" concept. A candidate who is closest to "all sides" – who is most moderate – may appeal to most voters to some degree, and may be least frowned upon by most voters.

But the second choice of most is not necessarily *anyone's* first choice.

The wild assumption of party leaders is that if someone bothers to vote for "their favorite Republican" in the primary, they will also vote for that candidate in November. But they have *no idea* why a person voted for that Republican.

It may be that "of all Republicans" he's their favored candidate, but they don't really want a Republican at all (Democrat voters are most likely to vote as a Republican in an open primary when there is no contest for the Democrat nomination – why not, right?).

It may also be that the Democrat is making a calculation (and many "thought leaders" on the left encourage this) that a certain Republican will be easier for the Democrat to beat in November. Therefore they choose *that* candidate to run against.

It's like getting to pick who you're playing against in billiards – do you choose the pool shark to play against, or the easy guy?

But secondly, and perhaps more to the point, a candidate who is the second choice of a wide cross-section of voters is more than likely preferred because they *do not* have an overriding political philosophy. In the end, that's a bad recipe for choosing a candidate because it's like the person chosen has no ideas of his/her own. They most certainly are *not* well prepared to *defend* a political philosophy (Republican platform issues) which they don't especially agree with.

They end up either doing a bad job explaining their stands, or they run away from the party's ideas – trying to stay as far away as possible, and making the rest of us look bad in the process.

The same criticisms can be brought against the broader strategy of GOP leadership – they're using a flawed process to decide who is more likely to win in November.

Independent and moderate voters come in two breeds.

One type is just a more unattached version of a Republican or Democrat. They don't want to get pigeonholed, or don't want to have to make excuses for a party's positions or mistakes ("Don't blame me!"). But they typically vote for one party or another in every election because their views are closer to that party.

An open primary isn't very helpful with these independents because they still want to favor someone with a particular political bent.

The other type typically doesn't have a vision for how they want to improve America. To the extent they do, it's a vague notion that America would be best if no ideology had a corner on the political market, so that neither prevailing ideology can pass its ideas against the opposition of the others.

That kind of thinking is nonsensical, for the most part.

Moderate voters of this way of mind are essentially saying indecision and "muddling through" is the best form of governing.

And then these same people complain the loudest about a "do-nothing Congress" that doesn't ever get anything done!!!

Think back to Reagan. Nothing energizes a voting populace – people on your side, or in the middle, either way

– like a candidate who knows what he believes and can explain why he believes it.

That was why America *loved* Reagan!

Would Reagan *ever* have been chosen in an open primary? Well, he might have – he did win a two-way election in a landslide, twice. As a matter of fact, one of his biggest wins was in an open primary in 1976 where Texas Democrats crossed over and voted for him. It's possible some of them did it because they figured he'd be easier to beat than Ford. But then again, Reagan is special. He is the "Great Communicator." And we know he did pull in a lot of Democrats in the 1980 race.

I can't say this validates the open primary process. More likely it's simply a validation of how good Reagan was.

Part of why we choose candidates in primaries first is to create definition between the candidates – contrast – and also to ensure that the party's values are best represented by that candidate. *Open primaries defeat both of those purposes.*

Election victories can be the result of disgruntlement, the amount of money spent, the personalities involved, or (ideally) a contest of ideas. Without adequate contrast between the ideas of the competing candidates, you cannot win a contest of ideas.

In 2008 Republicans nominated Sen. John McCain largely because of the results of a handful of key states with open primaries. Prior to that he'd been polling below 10% (sometimes below 5%) and was Republicans' *least* favorite choice.

Nevertheless, *avoiding* a contest of ideas in November is much of the reason for the Establishment's strategy for choosing candidates via open primaries, and this ultimately drives their desire to train their own voters to accept second best.

I would suggest that open primaries are a losing proposition for the GOP in general, and for the conservative movement in particular.

INTENTIONAL VOTING

We're the party of ideas for a *reason*! We *have* ideas, and we're not reliant simply on spending more money or throwing out more mud.

Sidebar: Not Voting

As I mentioned earlier, some wrongly consider voting 3rd party as "not voting." That's unfair and petty.

But there is a real problem with conservatives and Christians not voting, or even refusing to register.

Some feel *empowered* by simply not voting.

I don't really even understand this mindset. If you vote for some offices, but not in races where unacceptable candidates are running, it's possible to see your vote as an "undervote," and that's quantifiable to a point. Politicos can assume that candidate was less attractive *for some reason*. But it's definitely not as obvious as voting third party.

Not voting makes your vote invisible. Analysts know you're probably there, but you're like Bigfoot – a mythical creature whose motivations are inscrutable and no one can claim to know much about.

Not voting sends only a passive message. Not a positive one. If it sends any message at all.

An analyst might conclude you're dissatisfied, but why?

The Establishment could just as easily conclude you were in another country, or didn't pay any attention to politics.

Or were dead!

Not voting at all sends the wrong message – that you don't care.

By voting 3rd party you tell other parties not just that you were disgruntled, but also why and what policy positions you felt were important enough to deny the major party your vote.

Sometimes, there really isn't any candidate for that office who we will feel we can morally vote for. In that case, vote the other offices, and leave that one blank, or write someone in. That will show up as an undervote, and is quantifiable, though can't be evaluated qualitatively.

If we intend to change this vicious cycle we've gotten into – the cycle we've been *trained* to stay in – we, the base of the GOP, need to undertake "intentional voting."

Voting with a specific purpose in mind.

We need to understand how to vote third party so our protest votes are both "readable" and countable.

Countable – quantitatively, but also qualitatively.

Chapter 4
Compromise Results In Bad Government

When you start talking about remaining steadfast on principles in politics, someone will always dismiss your point by saying you *have* to compromise.

You *have* to vote for the lesser of two evils, and you *have* to vote for the nominee of the major party that's closest to your views, regardless of how many divergent positions are held by the individual candidate.

That's a lot of coercion.

You don't *have* to do *anything*!

Yes, it's good if you do something – if you take part as an active citizen.

It's *best* if you vote intentionally – *for* someone, *for* the right ideas, not because you *had* to!

Surely, their position makes sense if we rely upon a traditional (superficial) understanding of party politics. Isn't it clearly best for someone who agrees with you on 70 percent of the issues to win, rather than someone who agrees with you on 10 percent?

Get a good grip on your chair before I say this.

Not always.

It depends what the other 30 percent is.

Are we talking about degrees of difference on "mere policy issues?"

Or are we talking about compromises which do violence to fundamental principles?

In Chapter 8, written primarily to Christians, I'll have a discussion about discerning "actual evil" against differences of opinion on "non-evil" things that may nevertheless have negative consequences. For now let's stick with the idea that voting for someone with different non-evil policy differences isn't the same as voting for a candidate who embraces actual evil to a lesser degree.

The "Advantages" of Majority Status

When people say "vote party first because it still benefits your principles," they're usually referring to the organizational advantage of having party majority and potentially more votes for what you want in the legislative chamber. That works at the state level as well as in Washington DC.

Beware – those who say this are often a lot like used car salesmen advertising a car is a "great value at that price." Sure – for *him*, maybe!

Of course, some of what they say is true. I'll get that out of the way first, because these are the talking points the "vote party first" people will mention.

It is true, in most cases, that having control of a legislative chamber is preferable to not having control.

When things get really screwed up and difficult to fix, there are some leaders who would prefer to let the other party take the blame than to take charge and struggle with fixing things. But that's a digression.

Certain important powers are wielded by the chamber leader – the Speaker of the House or President of the Senate – who has the authority and powers to drive an agenda using his "whips" (vote counters and intimidators of recalcitrant legislators) to keep party members in line.

It is due to this dynamic that a Republican chamber will sometimes vote for "moderately principled" legislation (an oxymoron – it's generally compromised legislation) if the chamber leader demands it.

It is also true that majority status allows the chamber leader to influence the chairmanship, membership and character of each legislative committee. He or she can also choose which committees get input on specific legislation – these assignments mean either it will get smooth sailing, or it's dead on arrival. These are all important means of controlling which legislation gets passed, or *how it gets modified* before moving on in the process.

But on matters of principle, or even matters of degree, a chamber leader who is opposed to your views, even as a member of your favored party, can actually be more of an obstacle to legislation you want because they can stymie or change anything you or your legislative allies want.

They can water down your legislation. They can even turn it into something antithetical to what you were trying to accomplish. They can also completely *block* your legislation, just as effectively as they can block legislation from the *opposing* party.

Some chamber leaders end up so compromised they will find Democrat legislation more palatable than what you'd prefer to see.

Moderates are considered "moderate" because of the many areas where they agree with the other party. In office, they're "swing voters."

Chamber leadership is elected by the members of the majority and minority parties, respectively, and if the party's members are mostly moderates, then the chamber leaders will be too.

Conservatives in these cases will be locked out of positions of power – sometimes denied any kind of influence whatsoever.

Principled legislation is not likely to progress through such a chamber, even if it's controlled by Republicans, if the party leaders are not also principled conservatives.

Look at the US House, under Speaker John Boehner (R-OH), for example, or the minority leadership of Sen. Mitch McConnell (R-KY) in the Senate.

Do you see conservative legislation being crafted or guided by them? Or do you see watered down versions of progressivism? Do you see a fighting spirit? Or is it just a show to make them look tough, only to have them cave soon after having won meaningless "concessions?"

Boehner recently described himself as Obama's "best friend," and people were pretty sure he wasn't joking. He probably meant the president was counting on him to coerce his party into voting for progressive-weighted "compromise" bills.

We've gotten higher budget caps, immigration "reform" proposals, bailouts, et cetera.

These leaders can be more effective *opponents* to a conservative agenda than if the chamber leadership was in the hands of another party. That "benefit" of your party controlling the chamber can be directed *against* your aims, instead of in favor.

So control of the leadership positions *is* important. That part is true.

The lie is one of omission.

If your side – your philosophical faction – doesn't hold those positions, then your *opponents* do, no matter if they're Republican or Democrat opponents.

Legislative Pack Behavior

Peer pressure exists within legislative bodies – the urge to conform to decisions made by respected peers, the schoolyard taunts of not being a team player, and the desire of other legislators not to be made to look bad.

When an otherwise principled legislator makes a pragmatic decision to support compromised legislation, he or she does not make this decision in a vacuum. It will affect the considerations of other legislators of like mind. If one legislator sees a compromised bill supported by a buddy who often votes the same, the second legislator will become more likely to rationalize the choice and support the compromise themselves.

This is a well-known dynamic in political bodies. Undeniable.

Furthermore, besides the potentially positive peer "follow the leader" example, there is a negative peer pressure familiar to most of us since primary school.

A legislator faces double pressure. On the one hand he's seen by leadership as "extreme" if he does not also compromise, perhaps even facing pressure from his own party or caucus leaders to support the Establishment position and be a "team player."

On the second hand, those legislators who have already agreed to compromise will resent the example being set by those legislators who refuse to compromise. "Are you too good for us? What are you saying, I've made a bad decision? I'm not as 'pure' as you?" These elementary taunts may be slightly more sophisticated in a statehouse, or in Congress. Nonetheless, they exist for certain.

It's pack mentality.

In the Colorado legislature, when I worked there, Rep. Joe Nuñez and a handful of other "budget hawks" would vote against every cost increase, no matter how many Republicans supported the extra spending. It was a matter of pride and principle for them. The government was spending too much money, and it needed to stop somewhere. The buck stopped with them, no matter how "needed" some new spending program was.

Sometimes other legislators stood with Nuñez, other times they voted for the compromise bill.

Compromise teaches compromise. It begets more compromise. When another legislator joins the crowd by compromising, it makes them all feel better. The more join in the compromise, the more it affirms the choice of the first compromisers. Once a bloc of legislators stops holding the line on a principle, others will follow.

Fellow legislators who compromised resented Nuñez' principled stand. It made them look bad for caving in, and it set a higher bar for receiving those taxpayer watchdog awards.

But no matter what it was, even in the face of gubernatorial lobbying, at least one or two legislators stood firm in the face of all the pressure. Many votes were 64:1. They got lots of criticism from their friends. Their rewards were an easy conscience, the support of key constituents, and recognition from taxpayer groups.

Again, I want to emphasize that compromise on "non-gateway" issues isn't evil. A conservative can sign onto some critically important budget items without forsaking principle. Sometimes money spent early prevents more money spent later – prevention, or contingency plans.

Reagan was a conservative except with military budgets, which he intentionally increased for a purpose that eventually ended the Cold War with the Soviet Union. It could be argued he saved the US money in the long run by defeating the USSR peacefully and introducing the "peace dividend."

It's when compromise becomes rampant or willy nilly that a legislator ceases to be a statesman and becomes just another cog in the wheel.

But Nuñez had chosen spending as one of his gateway issues. Things had gone too far, and he was standing in the gap. So to maintain his principles he had to hold the line.

Bad Behavior Creates Bad Legislation

You would naturally think that if a candidate agrees with you 70 percent more than his opponent, he will make you angry 70 percent less often.

This is not always the case.

How often will they make you blow your top because you trusted them and they stabbed you in the back?

Compromisers and moderates tend to split the difference very quickly – whether on the issue of abortion, or guns, or spending or any other issue.

Their differences by degrees of opinion can frustrate us even when they technically agree with us – just not to the degree we want.

Compromised candidates result in compromised policies, and may result in compromised chamber leadership.

Compromised chamber or bloc leadership *enforces* compromise and *prevents* principled legislation from passing.

This means if a majority of Republicans within a legislative chamber are moderates, or compromisers, the leadership will be primarily comprised of "their people" and principled legislation (i.e. legislation that is in complete alignment with the party platform) will be watered down or unable to progress, no matter which party controls the chamber.

In order to get their agenda items passed, a party's leadership in the legislative body will compromise and split the difference with opponents of the legislation in order to try to "pull in" more members from a rival faction, almost like the RNC tells Establishment candidates to do in order to pull in more votes at election time.

If the principled faction were trying to pass a total ban on abortion, for instance, the pro-choice Republicans would never vote to support a ban on abortion. That's just not the kind of discipline exercised in Republican caucuses.

The Democrats sometimes compel their members to vote for something against their conscience (today's Democrat Establishment has far more confidence they have the power to replace recalcitrant members with new "toe-the-line" people in the primary – it works because candidates realize they can be replaced that easily because there's less discussion and citizen involvement in Democrat primaries, and because so much of Democrat campaigning relies on epithets and character assassination).

Republicans can be compelled by leadership to vote against their conscience, but in practice it's almost never when the issue is a principled stand.

Ostensibly conservative Republicans are famous for caving into pressure by leadership to compromise. But when a conservative is trying to get votes from the "swing voters" (RINOs) in his or her delegation, the moderate voting bloc will demand changes in exchange for their vote.

The majority leadership, if they don't have the votes to pass principled legislation, will almost always (read: always unless there is a voting bloc watching their actions and holding them accountable) compromise with the moderates in their party.

So, to re-emphasize, if your *principled faction*, not just your party, does not control a majority of the Republican votes in a chamber, then your party "controlling" that chamber is of no use to your principles.

It's not just a matter of moderates vs. conservative candidates and officeholders. Often, even conservative legislators will turn to compromise in order to achieve what they believe is a closer status to their ideal. In their eyes they're "moving the ball forward," even when in reality their compromise undermines their ideal, making it less likely to achieve in the future.

The worst part of this is that compromise becomes habitual, even for well-meaning conservatives.

Have you ever helped strong conservative candidates get elected to higher office, only to find a few years later they've become just like the compromising milquetoasts you wanted them to replace?

Many Republicans understand this frustration today, as leaders who cultivated votes from fiscal conservatives and anti-immigration voters and they're now working with the President on amnesty, or compromising on raising the debt ceiling to ever higher and higher levels. We saw the same thing – from many of the same officials – when the bailouts were under consideration.

Those who compromise their beliefs in order to achieve what they see as a partial victory are always angry at those who won't compromise their beliefs, because it suggests that *they* had an obligation not to compromise. Those who hold steadfast put *pressure* on those who compromise, and they don't like it.

So it's always easier for the compromisers if they can use every tool at their disposal to trick, manipulate or browbeat others into compromising.

This compromise dynamic, and the pressure from other legislators that drives it, is how the degradation of good people happens.

They compromise on one thing – often under intense pressure from party leaders, chamber leaders, or big donors. Soon it becomes easier and easier. It becomes a way to get things done. Not for the betterment of society, and not for the realization of principle. Instead, they learn to get things done for their friends around Washington, or their fat cat donors, or "their" compromised Republican president.

They enjoy the adulation and attention, not to mention the powerful positions or campaign cash offered as payoffs, showered upon them for being part of the "good old boys club."

Legislators who compromise on one issue are usually the ones who will compromise on others, because if it's "how to get things done" in one respect, it works in others.

And, eventually, those compromisers rise into leadership positions so they become the ones pressuring new legislators to support *new* compromise.

Compromise Gets *What* Done???

We've been told over and over – *trained to believe* – that compromise is necessary in order to get things done.

Compromise is necessary in some circumstances. And compromise isn't always bad.

See – I got myself to say it.

But only if that compromise doesn't *undermine* a key principle or violate fundamental rights of life or liberty.

I've heard otherwise smart individuals mock those of us who use the "slippery slope" argument, as if it's the stupidest thing anyone's ever heard of.

If you're trying to destroy principle there's never any more effective tactic than to nip away at the edges of the principle by proposing "a few, harmless compromises."

Compromise is how you break down a principle, not how you "build it back up."

If you're trying to pass gun rights legislation, and you have to compromise on it, you simply end up with a lesser infringement of the 2nd Amendment.

Make no mistake – once you make those small deviations from a fundamental principle (think in terms of "little obstacles" like the Constitution), broader compromises themselves seem more practical, and defenders of principle seem all that much more shrill and unreasonable in standing against "progress." Especially when longtime allies have thrown in the towel and joined the crowd, expecting you to do the same.

But, because of the nature of principle vs. compromise, compromise will never get you back to the principle. Never. Ever.

If each step you take back toward the principle only gets you half way there, you will never get there.

Restoring that principle again, once it's lost, requires a quantum leap in thinking – a reassessment and rejection of the "reasonable" compromises in the first place.

In my next book – on the pro-life Personhood strategy – I will make the case that trying to "compromise back to principle" can actually reduce your likelihood of ever reaching that ideal at all (because no compromise actually contributes to a debate on the basis of principle).

In a logical sense supporters find themselves arguing *against* the principle simply by the nature of supporting a compromise.

Independent observers begin to doubt if you actually believe in the principle at all, since you're essentially arguing against it, and wonder if maybe you're just a hypocrite.

The result of such compromises may be closer to your ideal, *depending how you figure it*, but it is never your ideal.

This is why, in US History, northern anti-slavery politicians were never able to pass principled anti-slavery legislation. They generally used "lesser of two evils" thinking to allow the extension of slavery into new territories, so long as they got something out of the bargain – a trade-off allowing a ban on slavery elsewhere. They patted themselves on the back for excluding slavery from some new territories even while *literally extending it* to some other new territories!

They were not speaking *against* slavery when they made these compromises! They were opposing it in the North and *supporting* it in the South. "Keep it down there, where it belongs!" They could not successfully argue that Blacks should be free, so long as they were assigning territories where bondage would continue.

When I speak, in a later chapter, specifically to Christians, this is part of my concern.

How are we, as Christians, to fight against evil if we (legislators or voters, either one) are endorsing compromise that may mitigate the evil in one respect, but endorses it in a different context? How can we morally pass legislation that "saves some babies" while at the same time that legislation endorses the continued murder of others?

Many Christians see this as a "net good." I argue that we must re-evaluate and change our strategy to avoid endorsing evil practices and teaching society the lesser of two evils is okay.

The Double-Minded & Turncoats

It's bad enough when we elect Republicans who vote with the Democrats on more than a handful of non-controversial things.

What about when they vote with the Democrats on *matters of principle?!*

There are many famous examples of rogue Republicans going the complete opposite direction on major party agenda items.

Anyone who listened to Rush Limbaugh for any of the decade prior to 2008 knew that Senator John McCain was a pinko, communist, lying, unprincipled, "might as well be a Democrat" liberal who every conservative loved to hate. He was famous for his "aisle-crossing" votes.

What "changed our mind" (literally or figuratively) in 2008?

He promised to be different.

Plus, Christians and Christian leaders told other Christians we had to support him or else we'd get someone worse.

It gets so you figure they might as well switch parties.

Some of them have.

Remember Republican Senator Arlen Specter?

You know... the guy who was in that Pennsylvania senate seat before *Democrat* Senator Arlen Specter?

President Bush, in 2004, went out of his way to campaign for this liberal agitator, Specter, against conservative primary opponent Pat Toomey, and the election was close enough that Bush's support was probably the only thing that kept Specter from losing to his conservative challenger (it was nearly a 50/50 primary).

In the general election, conservative Republicans held their nose and supported the party nominee.

Shortly thereafter Specter was lecturing the President from his Judicial Committee chairmanship on what kind of judges he was "allowed" to appoint, and giving him all kinds of griping and grief, right up to the point in 2009 where he switched parties to the Democrats.

And we're told we're always better off supporting the party's nominee, no matter how compromised he is?

Conservatives had gone out of their way to respect and support Specter. They massaged his ego by placing him in even more powerful positions of power.

Specter showed his appreciation by switching parties, benefiting the Democrat vote situation in the Senate, and earning even *better* concessions from *them*!

But if conservatives hadn't voted for "way less conservative than we would like" Specter, we would have had somebody worse, right?

Just like by not voting for Romney we got somebody worse in Obama.

Right?

In a coming chapter we'll address this – how winning with the wrong candidate is sometimes as bad or worse than losing.

Chapter 5
Only Nixon Could Go To China

You think nothing could be worse than losing?

Without winning the election, it's impossible to achieve anything you want, right?

So you have to win even if you have to do so with a candidate of "lesser evil." Right?

That's what we've been trained to think.

Hold onto your hats and prepare yourselves for a paradigm shift.

As we've just illustrated, sometimes the victory of a compromiser whose opinions are closer to your own than their opponent can be far more detrimental than someone who categorically disagrees with you.

The Republican President or Governor you just elected by holding your nose could be the worst enemy to conservative legislation!

How can that be, for real, though? It just doesn't make sense.

Not at first, anyway.

A once-popular saying was, "Only Nixon could go to China."

It refers to President Nixon's diplomatic overture to the People's Republic of China. He successfully switched communist China from being a tentative ally of the communist Soviet Union to being a third party rival to check Soviet power.

A Democrat could never have opened the door to Communist China, because in the heat of the Cold War they would be met with a war cry of "Treason!" from anti-communists back home.

But President Nixon's bona-fides on anti-communism were well established. He was "inoculated" – he could make a deal with China without Republicans coming out to oppose him.

It wasn't just because he was anti-communist. A Democrat known to be an anti-communist would probably still face Republican opposition.

Nixon could do it because he *was* a Republican, and most opponents of China were too.

Some of you might remember the quote was referenced in one of the Star Trek movies. Spock's point was that only Captain Kirk could make peace with the Klingons because he was known to be their worst enemy.

I'm not saying peace with China was a bad thing. Or even the Klingons. That's another whole discussion.

But this analogy applies to other things, and it's the root of why a bad Republican can be more dangerous in victory than a Democrat.

The Cowardly Lions of the GOP

The "Only Nixon could go to China" analogy has been clearly outlined in recent history.

President George W. Bush was able to get conservative Republican congressmen to compromise on immigration, spending, Medicare D, et cetera, in ways they never would have before.

These sure weren't part of their campaign promises when we elected them!

President Bush, with Medicare D and the first round of bailouts, passed the two most expensive, most statist, government entitlements in world history. And he did so *with the support of many Republicans!* They joined with some Democrats in support.

How did a conservative Republican Congress vote for more spending? Income redistribution? More entitlements? More big government programs?

They were asked to do so by a sitting president from their own party.

It's not just Republicans who have a brain transplant when their party takes the White House.

Millions of Democrat voters and Congressmen were vehemently anti-war prior to 2009. Anyone who didn't want to immediately bring the troops home from the "War For Oil" was a warmonger and traitor to the country. But in 2009 when Obama continued to fight the war in Iraq, and still yet after 3 more years of war, those same people thought President Obama was a hero!

"Look at how he's 'winning the War on Terror!' Yaay!"

All those Democrat senators who opposed every attempt the Bush White House made to win in Iraq and Afghanistan suddenly switched in 2009 to supporting *their* president's attempts to win in both conflicts. That includes Sen. John Kerry (D-MA), who now, as Secretary of State, is prosecuting wars in Afghanistan, Iraq and Syria!

But it's okay – these are Democrat wars now.

What? Did they have a frontal lobotomy?

No – the only thing that changed was what party occupied the White House and whose supporters had a vested interest in backing their chosen guy.

Then there's the flip side...

Rabid Wolverine Conservatives – Grr!

Remember how Republicans hated Bill Clinton? He was the worst guy ever to hold the office, right? But because Republicans hated him, Republican congressmen were motivated to stop his every effort! They were able to keep him from doing the worst that he intended.

Republicans had *spirit* back then! They would fight! Remember the filibusters? The government shutdown? The special prosecutors?

Conservatives made Clinton's life hell. Three quarters of what he wanted to do was stopped dead in Congress, including HillaryCare. The quarter he *did* accomplish was the least damaging.

And, going back to Bush's socialist entitlements, keep in mind that some Democrats still opposed him out of "principle."

Because opposing the Republican president was what they felt they had to do, even if they agreed with his policy and was playing their game!

That works the same with Republicans too – our Republicans in Congress will be there to fight Obama on most things, but they would have caved if McCain or Romney had asked them to do the *very same things*.

By and large, these were the same people – the same Congressmen, in many cases, were Rabid Wolverines back in the '90s and Cowardly Lions in the '00s.

Team Players Do What the Coach Says

The difference was made by who was in office – whether the President was a Democrat or a Republican. A friend or an enemy. Someone they should fight or defend and support.

Congress' ideology didn't change – it was still "moderate to conservative," but when Obama was in office Republicans were "conservatives" and fought against him, whereas when

Bush was in office these same Republicans were "moderates" and would support the President, almost no matter what was asked.

They became moderates because the President was moderate. And when the President asked for "some socialism" *they became socialists so they could support "their" President.*

Could President McCain have accomplished more of Obama's socialist agenda than Obama has?

John McCain was clearly to the left of Bush. And Bush had pushed socialist entitlements, so...

What might McCain have done?

President McCain corralling Republicans into an immigration compromise?

President McCain pressuring Republicans to compromise on the destruction of human embryos for research purposes? President McCain pushing a bevy of "reasonable" restrictions on gun ownership?

What about Romney in 2012? Again, Romney was clearly to the left of Bush, with his "moderate socialist" policies.

What might Romney have done to "out-do" Bush's socialist measures?!

The Republican Congress had pretty much promised to the American people that if they had the power to do so they would "repeal Obamacare."

But Romney practically *designed* Obamacare!

It was closely modeled on Romneycare — a coercive socialized healthcare entitlement program Romney implemented in Massachusetts. Romneycare required everyone to sign up, had penalties for not doing so, canceled plans that didn't fit with the program. *It even provided taxpayer funding for abortion on demand, with a $50 copay to the mom.*

What might President Romney have done to push socialism and drive compromise?

What would Republican congressmen, who had promised to "repeal Obamacare," do when asked to "modify" Obamacare instead to be more like Romneycare?

"We can't tell the president no. He's our party's president!"

Might we have watched President Romney reinforcing the idea of Obamacare, changing it slightly to fit his own model, and leaving the American people saddled with a form of socialized healthcare and the associated burden on taxpayers? For generations to come?

I swear to you – Romney would never, *ever* have repealed Obamacare.

It would have meant repudiating his own record!

President Bush passed two massive entitlement and spending programs. Romney was *clearly* to the left of President Bush.

And Romney was 100% a corporatist, not a conservative or capitalist. We might have seen yet *another* round of massive taxpayer bailouts to corporations.

Americans and legislators of both parties have been trained to support whatever "their president" wants, no matter how antithetical it is to their own personal or party principles.

So I have to ask... And I'd hope you would also be open minded enough to ask yourself.

When Romney lost, did we narrowly miss catching a bullet?

Moving the Ball Forward?

This is where I'm going to lose some of you. I know – I've watched it happen.

We've all been trained to think, *"Anybody's* better than so & so!"

Conservative Republicans have been trained for too long to see the victory of moderate candidates as "moving the ball forward." Supposedly we're always going to be better off if we've got a Republican in office, no matter how bad he is, because he's always going to cause less *damage* than the Democrat.

What about the economy and foreign policy? Wouldn't those two points alone make Romney a better president?

I won't contest that the world might be a *safer* place – Romney's not a total idiot (not like some presidents).

I won't contest that the economy would probably improve, with more jobs, etc.

But on the long term, who knows? I've never seen a socialistic economic plan work except on the short term.

Couldn't we have been so much better off, even if we had to somehow accept a modified version of Obamacare?

Wouldn't that "move the ball forward" in terms of being better for conservative philosophy than what we got – a second term for Obama, who opposes everything we want and tries every other week to eviscerate the Constitution?

Conservatives have to think of politics in terms of chess, not checkers.

Long term thinking can overcome and overwhelm apparent short-term defeats.

My modest proposal is that sometimes winning with a bad candidate can be worse than losing, no matter if some things would end up better in the short term.

I know we've been trained to reflexively scoff at this sort of suggestion – to immediately argue against it – but I ask you to hear me out.

Winning Doesn't Always Mean Victory

President Carter's four years in office helped Republicans far more than they ever helped the Democrats. It was a colossal failure – instead of validating Democrat ideas, he seemed weak and incompetent. He was jaw-droppingly inept at anything but causing chaos.

He did the Democrats no favors. None at all.

Carter *energized* Republicans!

Worse, he riled up independents to vote for Republicans.

President Carter made millions of Americans wonder why they'd *ever* voted for those lousy Democrats.

President Obama is energizing Republicans now. You know that – you've seen the kind of energy and fevered activity in conservative circles!

You and your friends are more determined to get rid of Obama and the Democrats than you were in the '90s when the Clintons were in office.

Consider this for a moment...

Without the disappointments of the Carter Administration – without stagflation and a series of foreign policy failures – there might have been no President Reagan.

The revolution which occurred in 1980 as Republicans, independents, moderates and Democrats placed conservative bomb-thrower Ronald Reagan in office was driven by popular disgust with "the best that Democrats could do" under Jimmy Carter.

The country saw how miserably Carter's liberal policies had failed. They were demoralized by foreign policy failures and a diminishment of US power and prestige.

The American people turned Carter out of office in a landslide!

The same *could* have happened in 2012. *Should* have! *Would* have, if Americans had had a candidate worth voting for.

And I expect it *will* happen in 2016.

But only *if* we have a candidate who presents a clear contrast with Hillary Clinton, or whoever the Democrat standard-bearer might be.

We didn't lose everything in 2012, with Romney's loss.

Besides possibly "missing a bullet," the American people and conservatism not only survived, but the country has *strengthened* in its opposition to Obama's policies.

If Americans were tired of Obama in 2012 – so tired that only a handful of his own tepid supporters would even bother to go meet "their President" at a campaign event – by 2016 think how much *more* tired Americans will be of this man and his policies.

Obama Hurts Democrats in 2016

The media wants us to think Hillary Clinton presents a clear break from Obama. She has "fresh, new ideas!" She isn't stupid on foreign policy! She'll fix the problems with Obamacare! She'll make us proud to be Americans again!

Please.

Clinton's ideas aren't any different from Obama's. Bill Clinton had some degree of independence from the culture of socialism that's pervaded the Democrat Party since the '70s. But Hillary is a died-in-the-wool socialist radical, and has been since college. New ideas?

She'll have as hard a time pretending she's a moderate as Romney had pretending he wasn't.

Foreign policy? She's partly responsible for many of Obama's foreign policy failures. She was probably behind some of her husband's foreign policy idiocies.

She may pretend, and the media may look the other way, but Clinton's claim to have a third way on foreign policy doesn't meet the laugh test.

Obamacare has many of the same tenets of Hillarycare. She's got a ball and chain there, too.

Pride in country? Again, she has some of the same liabilities as Obama – a lack of passion and respect for what America really stands for.

Going into 2016, the voting public is going to be twice as tired of "progressivism" (socialism) as they were in 2012.

That's exactly the time to present them with *real* fresh ideas, such as have not been loudly voiced in Washington since Reagan and Gingrich, 20 and 30 years ago.

The Man Who Would Be King

Maybe the most potent and heartwrenching point in favor of voting party first in 2014 is constitutional.

"If we don't vote Republican, even if we can't stand the guy, there's not going to be a country left in 2016!"

Well, I heard that in 2012, too. And now it's 2014, and we're half way there, and we still have a country. Frankly, I heard the same thing in 2008, and we were still there in 2012.

I've also heard people say 2016 (or 2014) will be our last chance to turn away from the brink. Now that most Americans are "on the federal dole," they'll never choose to go back.

Single party dominance in elections. Dependence forever.

Communism.

But after the Soviet regime and Warsaw Pact client governments fell – communist or hyper-socialist systems, all of them – the people of those countries elected some of the most conservative replacement governments in the world!

They went from total dependence to freedom and free enterprise. Poland, today, is less socialistic than Spain or Italy. Maybe even than Germany.

I've heard that with amnesty potentially bringing all these young Hispanics into the ranks of voting citizenship, Republicans will never win another election. Yes, I can see many of those immigrants voting Democrat for a generation just because they owe their citizenship to the Democrats (Republicans are being stupid if they think we can "run to the left" of the Democrats and get credit for their citizenship – you can't out-left the leftists).

I'm not convinced there, either. Free enterprise and the American dream are very powerful – more powerful to many than is dependency. New immigrants, no matter from where, are going to want to build a future for their families. Men also have a strong need to be actively employed – it's a matter of pride.

I have worked in situations where I see immigrants – some of them likely here illegally – working very hard for their money. Some of the hardest working people I know. As a Republican, I have a hard time imagining all of these people voting for socialist policies merely because of a party's stand on illegal immigration.

I'm not defending amnesty – illegal is still illegal – but I recognize some truth in what Gov. George W. Bush (R-TX) said before he was President. "Someone who will walk 300 miles for a job is someone I want working in Texas."

I don't see that population remaining Democrat forever.

Young Hispanics are also shown in polls to be fairly conservative in many of their attitudes. Add that to the fact that Hispanic culture is also reasonably conservative in some ways. These are inroads that can be used to build a conservative base within Hispanic culture, no matter how many millions of people come into the country.

It's true, Obama has proved he can successfully ignore the Constitution. And, yes, someone – Congress and/or the Supreme Court – is going to have to step in and slap him down or else we may never recover.

I once undertook an academic study of three republican constitutions – the United States' compared with those of Germany and Japan in the 1920s and '30s. Germany's Weimar Constitution, which preceded Adolf Hitler's dictatorship, ceased to work because their chancellors began to rule by decree, and the force of law presented by their constitution was lost. The breakdown of foreign constitutions was not strictly comparable to use of the kind of Executive Orders President Bush used, nor the kind that Obama has so far used, but if Obama is allowed to continue using them for more and more expansive powers, that becomes parallel.

But in a real sense the Constitution suffered some vital wounds even prior to Obama. President Woodrow Wilson did violence to Constitutional principles by introducing federal entitlement programs. President Franklin Roosevelt stomped all over the Constitution by implementing a whole array of socialist welfare and work programs, some of which – Social Security, for one – still exist today. The "Great Society" programs of the '60s only expanded across the foundation laid by Wilson and Roosevelt.

Even if we roll back every anti-Constitutional abuse Obama has exercised, we've still got some serious work to do in returning to Constitutional principles.

Yes, there is a real concern that Obama harbors authoritarian – even dictatorial – intents.

The best antidote to such ambitions is vigorous political opposition to his power grabs, a Legislative and Judicial branch each willing to stand up against him, and the continued loyalty of the US military to Constitutional principles.

Without either the military or the vast majority of the population to support him, any would-be dictator won't get very far in the United States, even today.

But, honestly, who's going to oppose Obama's executive power grab from the Establishment side? How is voting for Establishment politicians going to stop Obama any more (which is to say, barely, at all) than a Republican House already has under Establishment Speaker Boehner?

The Establishment treats the Constitution like it's "so much noise." Remember, these are the "perfect is the enemy of the good" people. Are they going to let the Constitution stand in the way of what they "know" America needs?

The Republicans *least* likely to oppose Obama's power grabs are moderates and Establishment Congressmen. You cannot count on someone who shares some of Obama's ideas on statism or liberty to "stand in the gap" against those threats.

Even if no Establishment officials harbor their own ambitions for greater extra-constitutional power, their leaders and officials do not truly understand Constitutional principles or the threats against them enough to fight against tyranny.

So it's not a valid argument to support them because we expect them to "save us" from the destruction of our Constitution!

Only by electing men and women of solid principle to Congress – people who understand the value of the Constitution and its guarantees – will our leaders be willing to stand up against Obama, or anyone else.

Vigorous Opposition

Thankfully, even with Establishment leadership, we've seen the "wolverines" in Congress at times.

Sometimes we've seen real, energetic opposition to his policies. More rarely, to his abuses of power.

Today's GOP Congress needs more "Gingrich" and less "Boehner" in choosing their behavior. Given that, it's exactly how Republicans can avoid the nightmare scenarios shown above, no matter who the next president is.

Vigorous opposition works when a GOP Congress stands against a Democrat president. More effectively, even, than when they stand against an Establishment Republican president.

I have hope that, with Tea Party help, and the results of intentional voting, the next Congress would be willing to stand up against either party's president, if they tried to go off the reservation.

Even more hopefully, I expect it's possible to avoid having a president that would require such a watchdog stance.

You may recall President Obama came into office promising "health care reform" and the Freedom of Choice Act (FOCA) to make abortion-on-demand part of his revised "American Dream."

But Republican opposition – spurred on and sustained by the visceral fear and outrage of conservatives – stopped most of what he wanted to do. Every Republican voted against Obamacare in a remarkable display of unity and discipline.

FOCA never happened. Roe v. Wade is still "the law of the land" but it hasn't been strengthened by Obama, other than Obamacare's requirements with regard to abortion coverage in health care plans. But that, itself, has been partially rolled back by the Supreme Court's Hobby Lobby decision.

And you have to admit, Obamacare's passage, and the methods used to accomplish it, contained within it the seeds of its own destruction. The Democrats pushed it over the top, but it had no momentum by the time it got there. Realistically, the only way it was a victory is if Republicans, or a Republican president, allow it to remain in law.

Vigorous opposition to authoritarian and progressive policy can be a victory in itself until such time when we can replace those progressives of either party with Republicans of the correct conservative stripe.

Besides, we won't necessarily avoid tinhorn authoritarians simply by electing Republicans. Can you swear, without an ounce of second-guessing, that no Republican would ever aspire to do the same as Obama?

Abuse of the tools of power is an outcome caused by human nature and the nature of power structures. Local governments and HOAs, even in conservative neighborhoods, often provide the worst examples! Eminent domain? Seizure of personal property so it can be "repurposed" to produce more tax revenue in the hands of the politicians' friends? That's corruption and corporatism as exercised by your own neighbors at the local level!

Honestly, can you trust someone who thinks it's okay for the federal government to force every American to buy a health care product (which is how Romneycare would have translated at the federal level) to follow the Constitution where it might limit what he can do?

Failed Leadership Works Both Ways

It's not just the failed policies of Carter's or Obama's progressivism that can have a negative impact on elections.

The failure of Republicans – even if that failure is due to a corporatist, "Republican progressivism" – may have an impact on future elections too.

Failure – especially the hypocrisy of the Establishment – will tarnish the Republican brand.

Many Republicans argue that by the end of his eight years, President George W. Bush had hurt the cause of the Republican Party through the way he conducted the War on Terror.

Thanks to Democrat sound bites and the way the media pilloried Bush on a daily basis, by 2012 grassroots Democrats came to see him as Satan. He'd lost the support of a lot of Republicans too, as evidenced by the strength of Rep. Ron Paul's supporters as a GOP counterculture.

The state of the economy in 2008 sure didn't help Republicans. Voters typically turn out the party in power when they are fretting about the economy, and in 2008 jobs and our economic future weren't looking so hot.

It wasn't "all Bush's fault" as some would claim.

But the mere impression of an economy on life support, bolstered by the unprecedented handout of trillions of dollars to prop up corporation and industry, made Americans wonder if we were on the verge of another Great Depression.

In 2008 elections the economy worked *against* Republicans. Campaigning on "jobs and the economy" was a lot harder back then, considering many Americans blamed Republicans, rightly or wrongly.

By contrast, Reagan's 8 years of conservative leadership left Republicans in good stead.

Is the difference Bush's "progressivism lite" vs. Reagan's sincere conservative leadership?

So, again, let's think in hypothetical terms about how a McCain or Romney victory might have been concretely worse for conservatism and the country than what most Republicans ever expected.

Could the failure of either, due to their rejection of conservative principles, have made the country worse?

Could they have even "killed" conservatism?

Leaders Train Their Supporters

Let's talk about Rep. Ron Paul (R-TX) for a moment (not to be confused with Senator Rand Paul (R-KY), who seems to be very different in a number of ways from his father).

I know and respect a lot of Ron Paul supporters. I set them aside from the Ron Paul fanatics. There are a lot of good reasons to have supported Ron Paul. But his foreign policy proposals were something I could never get my head around.

I was raised during the Cold War. So were many of you. It would have been hard for me to imagine, as a teenager, or even as a twenty-something in the '90s, a strong and vocal minority of Republicans opposing US bases in other countries.

That was always a Democrat thing – "Close down the NATO bases in Germany! Bring our troops home! Stop antagonizing the Soviet Union!"

Most of us never doubted that if the United States military hadn't been kept reasonably strong – if Reagan hadn't rebuilt the American military and had bases near strategic flashpoints around the globe – that the pre-Gorbachev Soviet leaders would have taken every advantage and expanded imperially.

It's called geopolitics. The world is a dangerous place, full of anarchy kept at bay only by the collaboration of alliances of great nations.

When Hitler took over continental Europe, the United States was weak. If the US hadn't become strong again, Hitler might have won World War II.

Without the United States, evil might have won.

During the Cold War the USSR was the real threat to world peace.

Perceived American weakness invited Premier Khruschev to try tipping the scales by placing nuclear weapons in Cuba in 1962, right on America's doorstep.

That took heady aggressiveness. It was a hugely antagonistic move! The same could be said of the USSR's 1979 invasion of Afghanistan. They weren't an idle threat.

History demonstrates that when the US fell down on the job and appeared weak, as it did during Carter's Administration, and other times before, the Soviets took advantage and continued to expand their empire.

All this to say, history proves the geopolitical principle that power abhors a vacuum, and in the absence of a balance of power and the vigilant defense of a nation's interests through diplomatic and military strength, evil men will never miss a chance to advance their own interests at the expense of the less powerful.

Between World War II and the 1990s, geopolitical vigilance was a keystone of Republican policy. True, Republicans opposed "nation building" efforts by President Clinton in Bosnia and other places where a national interest wasn't apparent.

But that's not inconsistent with geopolitical vigilance. In fact, it support it, by not frittering away American strength on things that don't affect the United States' own security.

Today, in 2014, we have more than enough evidence that if the United States intends to remain secure, even within its own borders, we have to be strong enough to defend ourselves from enemies who are still abroad. It's made clear by an aggressive People's Republic of China, an expansionist Russia, and a new Islamic movement — ISIS — which threatens to turn the Middle East into a base from which to attack into the United States and Europe.

This "neo-conservative" epithet is a red herring. Keeping America strong, and defending its interests worldwide, wasn't a "neo-con" thing — it was a Republican thing. It was a sensible thing.

Geopolitics, too, is chess, not checkers. The game is to think several moves ahead and limit your opponents' present and future options.

All around the world our enemies are rattling sabers at us. Don't think they can't hurt us if we let our guard down.

How did some Republicans, in the 21st Century, suddenly decide the GOP should advocate disengaging from world affairs and letting other powers and other militaries take the initiative? Allowing them the freedom to frighten our allies and undermine our interests?

These Republicans adopted isolationist attitudes partly because Ron Paul *trained his supporters*. They wanted to defend Paul against criticism, so they had to defend his ideas too. All of them.

I have no objective evidence, but I'd be willing to bet that most of his *Republican* supporters (I specify because Ron

Paul had many independent, libertarian and Democrat fans too) adhered to Reaganite foreign policy assumptions until they decided to back Ron Paul. Most Republicans who chose to line up with Paul did so because of his attractive stands on economy and liberty issues.

It is also possible that many former Reaganites changed their views after watching the war in Iraq drag on. But I posit that most of Paul's legions began to oppose foreign involvement only after signing on with him. They learned to adopt his ideas because they wanted to be able to defend him against all opposition during the primary.

They could allow no chink in the armor. Anytime you're forced to admit, "Well, I really don't like his policy on this, but..." it makes it sound like you're backing the lesser of two evils, and no one likes to admit they're doing that, even if it's merely a training reflex.

It's for this same reason that, in 2009, all these peacenik Democrats started cheering for victory over the terrorists in Iraq. They had to back their guy, and their guy wasn't ending the war abruptly like they expected him to – the troops weren't coming home.

Rather than renounce their choice and admit they'd made a mistake, human nature makes it so much easier to just change your mind and go along.

These same people probably returned to their pacifist roots when Obama did finally disengage from Iraq, and are now probably doing backflips to try to rationalize airstrikes against ISIS.

Playing For All The Marbles

Power – especially the Presidency – would give Romney the opportunity to train his supporters.

At the 2012 Republican National Convention, a furor started when Romney and the Establishment Republicans forced through a rules change giving future nominees the power to largely tailor the GOP platform to their own ends.

That has for decades been a power of grassroots activists and delegates, which is the only reason Reagan's platform persists to this day.

To the best of my knowledge, that rule is still there. You didn't hear a lot about this in "mainstream" conservative media, because they were already carrying water for Romney. Little opposition to the move was generated except on strictly conservative websites and radio shows.

So, they're trying to silence conservative input into the platform, plus the Establishment is also actively trying to quash conservative Tea Party candidates in favor of Establishment picks.

Instead of raising money to oppose the Democrats, the Establishment has been raising money *specifically* to tip Republican primary contests. They "put out a hit" on Republican candidates they don't like in primaries around the country. There are a variety of political groups associated with moderate or progressive Republicans, including the "Main Street Partnership" (which is partially funded by socialist financier George Soros), the Republican Leadership Council and the Republican Majority for Choice (which no longer represents a "majority" of Republicans, if it ever did). Their purpose is to fund Establishment Republicans against Tea Party Republicans in the primary election season.

If you don't doubt the Republican Establishment thinks they're at war with the Tea Party and conservative values, consider that two of the PACs associated with the Main Street 527 are called "Republicans Who Care." As opposed to the rest of us?

That's the Establishment intentionally painting all other Republicans as extremists!

We've already mentioned the Establishment's tricky hand in the Mississippi senate race.

The Republican Governor's Association also involved itself in Colorado, laundering money through a proxy organization, by buying ads to defeat a Tea Party candidate for governor. As the Establishment either feels more threatened, or closer to victory, they will continue to ramp up these anti-conservative efforts through any means they can.

They have no interest in unity except when it's *their* candidates needing conservative votes.

It's war. They mean to get rid of us.

Taking Reagan's Portrait Down

Since the 1980s the whole Republican Party has paid homage to the memory and legacy of Ronald Reagan, the modern day "Grand Old Man of the Grand Old Party." The Establishment candidates work *against* Reagan's legacy behind the scenes, but their candidates all have to appeal to the memory of Reagan to wind up their base.

They *hate* it!

What if they could replace Reagan with a new poster boy? Someone more to their liking? Someone who could raise a new generation of Republicans to support a new wave of Establishment candidates?

Had Romney won in 2012, he would have been their guy. He still could be, in 2016. Or Jeb Bush. Or Chris Christie.

Romney could be painted as the savior who ended the ordeal of Obama and rescued a corrupted version of "conservatism" for a new century.

They'd have to call it conservatism. That's how they'd marketed Romney. But once he was in office they could re-define what conservatism means.

It's happened before – everything is relative. President Nixon was a statist who believed in price controls and large budgets, but he was considered a conservative at the time. He was part of the cadre of country-club Republicans who Senator Barry Goldwater decried in his groundbreaking 1964 manifesto, *Conscience of a Conservative*. He railed against how

Republicans had given up trying to cut the budget, and only increased spending at a slower rate than the Democrats.

Romney would be a Nixon style "conservative." To make it all stick, Reagan would have to be collectively forgotten. Easy enough with a younger generation of Republicans who don't remember anything about Reagan because they weren't even born yet.

Because he would be an incumbent in 2020, the whole party would then be engaged to re-elect Romney. Primary opponents would be tarred with accusations of disloyalty, because to challenge him would be to weaken the Republican president, making it more likely we'd get a Democrat.

Opposition to Romney's moves, or even mere criticism, would be stifled and smothered for the good of the party.

Could Romney Kill Conservatism?

The major conservative media outlets have abetted the process of Establishment ascendancy over conservatives within the party.

In 2012 they put out the word early that Romney was "the guy who could win," infecting many conservatives with that mantra. In 2014 there has been more rah-rah for Establishment candidates, and even open talk of Romney as nominee in 2016, which could easily turn into an idiotic repeat of 2012.

The "Main Street" 527 is just the start. Imagine a sitting president, with all his popularity and power, campaigning for every Establishment Republican on the primary ballot around the country.

To each adoring crowd, he'd say, "I want you to back 'Establishment Candidate X' because he's my friend and if you want to support *me*, you'll support them. I'm the President, and when I try to push for Republican policies I need allies, not someone who will get in the way and work against me. Right?"

Anyone who dared to back the conservative would be "not supporting *our* President."

Romney has already, in 2014, backed former Sen. Scott Brown (RINO) in a primary against a conservative in New Hampshire (Brown moved there after losing re-election). This is not an isolated case.

President Romney would get to train a new generation of supporters. Bush Jr. never got to do that. He had introduced the concept of "compassionate conservatism," but still ran on the memory of Reagan and fiscally conservative innovation. Plus, his family name was inextricably linked with the Reagan legacy. He could have *tried* to rebrand himself, but it wouldn't have worked.

With control over the party platform taken out of the hands of the grassroots, Romney could end the long tradition of stability – the Reagan platform of issues and stands that has survived since 1980, almost unchanged.

Any Establishment president *could try* this, but Romney has the charisma to really displace Reagan's image if he really had a mind to. Gingrich couldn't do that. Santorum couldn't do that. Rand Paul? Only for different, far more intellectual reasons.

But didn't I say earlier Romney came off in 2012 as a cold fish? A rich cold fish? Yes. But that's in the context of a nasty election cycle. Many Republicans couldn't see the charm of Barack Obama in 2008, but millions of other Americans saw it, and responded to it.

A sitting Republican president with Romney's charisma would have far more power over young Republicans and "party first" supporters after taking office than he would even on those same people before the election. There is an aura of majesty about the presidency that many citizens are susceptible to.

What if conservatives shouted, "Reagan!" and no one came?

His legacy stands for itself in an entirely intellectual sense. But he's been sustained in the public mind by the reverence of conservative Republicans and by those who lived through the '80s and remember how great they felt with a confident, steadfast leader at the helm of the American state.

That's not guaranteed to continue, and if Romney has a vested interest in taking over that mantle, he's going to try.

Those conservatives who agreed, in 2012, that Romney wasn't a sufficiently conservative nominee, usually said, "We'll get it next time. We'll put up a conservative against him. But right now we have to get him over the top."

These conservatives were afraid to stand up against Romney *then* – afraid they would hurt his chances, and he wouldn't win. How would they acquire the political, personal and philosophical courage to stand up against him four years down the road, when they would be told it was even *more* critical that a Republican win, to "keep the rollback of Democrat ideas running," and it would be an even *worse* time to say bad things that might keep him from getting re-elected?

He'd still be "the lesser evil who can win."

It's simply voter psychology. Without an "intervention," voter rationalizations toward compromise will be just as strongly held in later elections.

Chapter 6
Intentional Voting

So it's not about "getting it right the next time" – waiting until the next election cycle to get a conservative in office.

Once that Establishment poster boy is there in office – *nay*, as soon as that poster boy is the *nominee* – there won't be any critical mass of support remaining to really get rid of him. Conservatives who made apologies and carried water for him have become *invested*. He's an incumbent, and a huge portion of the party believes it's their job to support their party's incumbents, whether they agree with them or not.

We're acting like battered women, knowing that we're in a bad relationship but not knowing how to get away. Not even, in most cases, realizing that we do! We stay and support the GOP even though we're being horribly abused.

It's got to stop.

We have to fight that Establishment power.

How can we create real change and bring the party back to obedience to its own party platform?

We're already close to succeeding, even *without* a widespread, coordinated strategy of conservative "intentional voting."

We nearly did it in 2012, when first Herman Cain, then Rick Santorum, then Newt Gingrich took first place and appeared like the clear leader for the presidential nomination. And, no, it wasn't Romney's money that won it for him, or else he would have been the nominee in 2008, too.

In a real sense, 2012 showed our strength. Look how many supporters there were to go around. Enough to sustain (and fund) five major contenders for the conservative vote.

In the 2012 presidential primary the failure of the conservative movement was *not* being conservative. It was having too many candidates who stayed in for too long.

Then we blinked, and figured if none of our candidates could stay on top for more than a month then maybe the Establishment was right about Romney.

Ultimately that lack of focus cost us our greatest chance to take charge of the GOP from top to bottom, and allowed the Establishment to entrench its power and control through the leadership of moderate Mitt Romney.

If we don't focus our strategy and quit undermining ourselves it will take even more effort next time around to create the change we need and to bring conservatives back into control of the party. But how?

I believe a clue can be found in an Establishment attitude expressed by my former employer, Governor Bill Owens of Colorado. In the weeks after the tragic shootings at Columbine High School he undertook an effort to pass "responsible gun control measures" – infringements of gun rights he calculated wouldn't ruffle too many feathers.

The NRA supported him. Other gun rights groups didn't. A reporter asked him if he was concerned about losing the support of these angry gun owners.

Owens' response? "Who are they going to vote for, the Democrats?"

While it was clearly an unguarded moment, and a phrase he would rather have taken back, I'm sure it expressed his blithe confidence that he could take those votes for granted.

Attitude Adjustments – Ours and Theirs

Owens was confident in his circumstances. His supporters had been trained to support the incumbent, no matter what.

But that *attitude* is part of the problem we're wrestling with.

To fix the problem we have to change *our* attitude. *And theirs.*

In this day and age, when there are viable, principled third parties, it is foolhardy for candidates to assume the votes of conservatives and liberty activists are in the bag. Without a principled candidate to vote for, some will simply stay home, or vote third party.

This is *not* a bad thing for the conservative movement. In fact, It's the way our voice will be heard the loudest.

Party apparatchiks who are reading this, hold onto your seat, because I'm about to say the unthinkable...

Conservative Christians, fiscal conservatives and liberty conservatives of strong principle each have to be willing to "walk away" from a particular candidate, even if he or she is the party's nominee. Principled voters have to be willing to walk away from compromised candidates, *even if that means someone still more opposed to our ideas ends up winning.*

That's not "voting for the socialist" by proxy. It's not "voting for the pro-infanticide candidate." It's not "voting for the guy who's 100% opposed to gun rights."

It's voting for the opposite of all those things – it's fighting against the progressives and those candidates of the Republican Party who split the difference and cause things to get worse in America every day.

It's intentional voting.

It's using your vote as part of a calculated, forward looking strategy for conservative victory. Maybe that victory won't come in the current election cycle. But it has a better chance of happening than if we continue to muddle along through the Establishment's status quo.

What we've been doing – the "oops we lost the primary, better luck next time, but for now let's support the lesser socialist" strategy – isn't working.

Expecting that if we try it just one more time it'll suddenly work is silly, wishful thinking.

We've been undermining ourselves and our beliefs by voting for the people who oppose us inside our own party.

We've been making things worse.

Voting Our Values

Intentional voting is a better long term strategy, even if we may lose ground on the short term, we're building a better foundation for the future.

I'm not talking about a "purity party" – a gathering of idealists so small it can't win elections. What I envision is a party gathered around these popular core principles that 80% of Republicans already believe, and which when presented properly and received fairly by the general public have proven sufficiently inspiring.

Let the Establishment voters make the concessions and vote for principled candidates because they're better than the other party. The coalition of the current party structure can remain very much the same, the main difference will be who's in charge.

And we have to evangelize – we have to spread our coalition, using the powers of messaging and contrast and inspiration to draw in new people from other parties or even people who've never been involved in politics before. Politics is not a "zero sum game" and never has been. With work it's possible to generate new voters and new activists.

But to do that we have to go out and make the case for why conservative ideas are better. We can't hide our message and hope no one hates us for what they don't understand.

And we have to show the Establishment who's boss by voting our values – voting only for people who are on our team, not on their own.

The Party has to face real – painful – consequences for

trying to manipulate us. Even if tomorrow *we* feel the pain through inane leadership we'll have to fight all the way (I mean the Democrats this time, not the GOP Establishment).

Politicians must *fear* that if they don't take appropriate positions on issues outlined in the party platform they will lose the votes of this critical base of voters.

That's pressure politics.

For conservative principles to truly prevail, we voters who passionately favor those ideals must be empowered. We must regain confidence that we can pressure candidates and politicians into taking positions and making promises that they can be held to.

We have to exert *effective quality control* over our representatives in government, so they represent *us*, not the Establishment.

This is how we train our politicians!

The GOP Establishment must be allowed to fail, *not* pushed over the top by us on the strength of yet another set of empty promises.

Even if they're the only representative of the Republican Party still running.

That kind of retaliation is the only kind of language parties actively respond to.

We have to stop letting them train us.

We have to begin training *them*.

We do that by making them fear that without us they will lose.

In order to get that across we have to show them our willingness to walk away by putting on the pressure.

And if they still ignore us we have to punish them for doing so.

By walking away.

Otherwise, *they* still have the power, not *us*. And they will use that power to force us and our conservative philosophies into obscurity. They've already been trying.

The time is now! This strategy may not show results in one election cycle, which is why we have to continue the lessons to the GOP Establishment we've been teaching since 2006.

Don't blink! We have to keep it up until it works.

But we have to act.

Now!

Chapter 7
The Tea Party & Third Parties

There are two potential avenues to achieving conservative victory in America's political party structure.

People have been trained to think there's only one — gain control over the leadership and grass roots of your favorite major party. "If you can't do it, tough luck – you should support the party anyway because it's the only game in town and no third party will ever amount to anything anyway."

I want to state up front, this is *not* a "bash the GOP" chapter. I've voted third party or independent before, and I surely will again. But I still believe the Republican Party remains the more effective vehicle for enabling conservative ideas. I've known Libertarians who became Republicans so they could get elected, and who went on to greatly influence the direction of Republican policies. Many Republicans are sympathetic with those libertarian ideals. You just have to be able to overcome the Establishment to put them into action.

But it's important for us all – Republicans especially – to understand third parties and their role in our political process. It is a central prerequisite to dissecting many of the lies and untrue mantras we've been trained by the Establishment to believe.

Think back to Gov. Owens' statement – "Who are they going to vote for, the Democrats?"

No. They may very well vote third party instead. And they're not wrong for doing so.

The GOP Establishment has been assuming for years that Christians and other conservative voters won't vote for anyone but Republicans, no matter how miserable their candidates are on the major economic, social or liberty issues.

They were right, for about a decade. Now we've caught on, and we're not going to be taken for granted anymore.

We, as a conservative movement, have to stand up for ourselves and make our voice heard, or we will never get our power back.

It is important to realize how third parties and third party voting can become a lever we can use in our favor, for purposes of "intentional voting."

Third Parties Have No Influence

People have been trained to think third parties are ineffective and can't win.

By who? By the major party Establishments!

Both the Republican and Democrat Parties benefit by suppressing votes to third parties.

People don't vote for third parties because they think they're ineffective. People think third parties are ineffective because they don't win. Third parties don't win because people don't think they are effective. It's a circular argument that keeps third parties from recognizing their potential.

What most people don't realize is that a third party doesn't have to win to be effective!

It only requires them to gain enough votes or cause enough of a ruckus that major parties change their behavior and policy positions in reaction.

Major parties and candidates realize that if they face a serious threat from a third party they may lose just enough votes that they'll lose the election. And they know that unless they cater to the voters who might vote third party instead, their victory might be at stake.

So the great power of a third party is to *influence* the creation of policy in major parties, and among major party candidates. The stronger a third party is – the more votes it can move, and the more potentially popular it is – the more influence it has over major party policy.

The Green Party has exerted a great deal of influence over the Democrat Party in recent decades despite only occasionally fielding a candidate for major offices who carries any name recognition. They've moved the Democrat Party decidedly to the left on environmental and war issues.

"Third Parties Aren't a Consideration. Really. I Mean It. Stop Thinking About Them!"

One day, during the 2004 election cycle, I was listening to Randi Rhodes on the Air America radio network. At the time I was a solid supporter of George W. Bush's re-election. But, as a way of "checking myself" – of assuring that I don't fall into the trap of relying on only one perspective for news – I sometimes check out talk shows or websites opposed to my point of view. Air America was a Democrat-friendly radio project – sort of a wholly owned subsidiary, much as FoxNews is for Republicans. Their *job* was to promote Democrat candidates.

That evening, Rhodes was excited because she'd run into Patti Smith – a Vietnam era anti-war singer, and one of her heroes. She'd convinced her to come on the air with her. They talked for a while about how awful it would be if George Bush were re-elected and continued the war in Iraq, relating it to the Vietnam war Smith opposed. Then Rhodes turned the conversation to how wonderful John Kerry would be, and how he would stop the war (ironic, in light of his current role regarding Iraq and Syria). Smith sort of pooh-poohed Kerry, as if he was a wimp, and said she was supporting Ralph Nader, who had been the Green Party candidate in 2000, but was running with the Reform Party in 2004.

The whole character of the interview changed!

Rhodes, whose *job* it was to back John Kerry, had suffered the unintended consequences of inviting a guest on the air without thoroughly vetting her. Nader, at the time, was a real threat to Kerry – he was someone who could earn enough peacenik and enviro-wacko votes away from Kerry to cost him the election. Rhodes shut down the interview – she expressed shock at her guest's opinions, said Kerry was the candidate who could win, said he was the only candidate who could stop the war, and then her guest was gone.

Go to break, and as soon as Rhodes was back on the air she was talking about how stupid her "hero" was for supporting Nader.

That amusing illustration demonstrates the proof of my point. If Nader weren't a threat, they could have agreed to disagree on the air without an awkward blow-up. It wouldn't have been a big deal. But because a million likely Democrat voters were listening to Rhodes' show, she risked her guest convincing some of them – even a small percentage – to vote third party, and she knew *that* would be a disaster.

Such things are a concern every election cycle. If it weren't for the Libertarian Party, Republicans could be more free with their spending and fiscal policies. If it weren't for the American Constitution Party, Republican candidates could afford to ignore hotbutton Christian conservative issues. If not for the Green Party, the Democrats could afford to be more rational in their foreign policy speeches.

Third Parties Can't Win

So the main point is that third parties don't have to win to have significant influence on politics.

If all the people who preferred third party policy positions would actually vote for them, they might win!

But that's not to say they don't ever win anyway. Or come close.

Think of the amazing results from Colorado in 2013, where three popular recall efforts were mounted to displace Democrat legislators who had ceased paying attention to their citizens. The grass-roots uprisings that resulted in three state senators losing their jobs had a great deal in common with third party efforts.

102

The recalls weren't a third party challenge – they were run by Republicans and independents. But it makes the point.

When the major parties cease to respect their constituencies, their legislators are at risk, even in districts where their party has overwhelming advantages.

Reform Party candidate Jesse Ventura became Governor of Minnesota after the 1998 election. The Democrat candidate for governor, believing the myth that third parties cannot win, invited Ventura to enter the televised debates. He was betting Ventura would draw voters primarily from the Republican side. His move was too clever by half. The people of Minnesota appreciated Ventura's freshness, his ability to communicate, and the alternative he offered to major party hypocrisy and gridlock. Ventura won with 37% of the vote, eking out a victory by 3 percentage points (the Democrat only got 28%).

Rick Jore, a Constitution Party candidate, won a legislative seat in Montana (he had previously served as a Republican).

In a 2009 special election for Congress in New York the Tea Party contributed to the near-success of a candidate from the Conservative Party who ran as an alternative to the liberal Republican. Candidate Doug Hoffman garnered 46% of the vote, and only lost because the Republican dropped out and endorsed the Democrat instead.

The Constitution Party also acquired "major party" status in Colorado, following a peculiar circumstance in 2010 where their gubernatorial nominee – Tom Tancredo, a longtime Republican with nationwide notoriety on immigration issues – took second place, earning more votes than the scandal-ridden Republican.

The GOP, that year, cleared barely 10 percent of the vote, narrowly avoiding reclassification to "minor party" status!

It turns out that most third party candidates who achieve near- or complete success have prior name recognition from being major party officials.

But there's nothing to say this isn't the only way a third party could take positions of influence in the future. Party switching isn't unheard of. We've seen major officeholders switch parties when they see which way political winds are blowing.

Office holders from the Democrats and Whigs both switched to the Republicans in the 1850s. A decent third party could benefit from such a shedding today if major rifts opened up in one or both of the major parties.

Constitutional Obstacles

It's easy to make a convincing case for "you can only have two major parties in America – there's not *room* for a successful third party."

On the long term, there *isn't* room to sustain a third party in US politics. The U.S. Constitution is written in such a way that it encourages success for only two parties. The Electoral College system (which I support as foundational to states' rights – this is *not* a plea to get rid of it) is designed so that if no candidate for president gets more than half of the Electoral Votes the U.S. House of Representatives is called upon to decide who shall become president. Unless a third party has made significant inroads in Congress (it would require at least a third of the seats to be held by sympathetic Congressmen) then the major party members of Congress will naturally choose from their own party's bench.

So, except in the most unusual circumstances, Congress is not going to support a third party candidate for president, and otherwise a third party candidate would have to gain more than 50 percent of the Electoral Votes. Otherwise he or she is locked out of power.

However, there's nothing about the Constitution that says the two major parties have to be the Democrat and Republican Parties. They weren't always the major parties – things have shifted previously.

A Third Party Success Story

Here's a story I'm surprised not every Republican knows.

Some third parties in the 19th Century were formed around anti-slavery ideals.

During those years – the early 1840s up to the early 1850s – American presidents and Congressmen danced around the slavery issue in order to promote commerce, the economy, and to allow the Union to continue. Politicians on both sides either downplayed or gave lip service to the slavery issue in order to get elected. Slavery remained only in the background of political thought in Washington D.C.

Both major parties were home to anti-slavery factions which had little influence within the party. Anti-slavery voters were forced to choose between "lesser of two evils" candidates who didn't really care about opposing slavery, but were "better than the other guy."

Slaves lived and died in misery throughout the South, and even when they escaped to supposed freedom in the North, laws passed by these "lesser of two evils" politicians forced them to be captured and returned to their owners in the South (the Fugitive Slave Act).

But as anti-slavery voters became more confident and empowered, they began to support only candidates who regarded the slavery issue seriously, and who made promises to take action once they got to Washington.

They presented a challenge to the major parties – "Change, or else lose our loyalty!"

The leaders of the Whigs and Democrats decided they didn't need to earn those votes. It was an arrogant and unwise decision.

Did these anti-slavery voters lose their influence by dividing over matters of "ideal" principles and turning to pressure politics and intentional voting?

No. They began to drive the politics of the period.

One of those third parties came to dominate the politics of the next several decades. For 70 years, in fact, and for a great portion of the century afterward.

A mere six years after its first formation, the Republican Party elected its first president, Abraham Lincoln, on an anti-slavery platform.

Slavery was banned within just five years of Lincoln's election – just 11 years after the formation of the Republican Party, and just seven years after the U.S. Supreme Court had officially reaffirmed slavery as a legal American institution.

As an amateur historian, I look at the events of the 1840s through 1860s as a testimony to the sheer degree of change that can occur in public attitudes and political opinion within a relatively short period of time. What happened during that period cannot be pinned all on the Civil War. There were real shifts in public opinion.

Newt Gingrich reminds us that, "In November 1974 [due to Watergate] only 18% of the country identified as Republican. It's hard to believe that six years later Ronald Reagan won in a landslide and two years earlier Nixon had won re-election in a landslide. A note for those who think things can't change rapidly."

Here and elsewhere I'll say I believe such a shift of public opinion can occur today, and I believe it can be driven by recognition of the humanity of the unborn child. Abortion is the slavery issue of our day with this potential.

Don't discount any party. Properly endowed with a transcendent issue, it could change the world.

I would invite you to examine the last chapter of this book (after the conclusion – the preview chapter) to see what I believe is the transformational equivalent of slavery in today's politics – protecting the Personhood of the unborn child.

The Libertarian Party

The Libertarian Party is the largest, best organized and most effective third party in the US. It stands for many of the same things the conservative wing of the Republican Party stand for. Therefore it's often assumed to "draw votes from" the Republican candidate.

But that's a superficial assumption – that if the Libertarian candidate weren't there, all those votes would go to a Republican.

The Libertarian Party also draws from Democrats, because of its typical pro-choice position on social issues – abortion, marijuana, etc. Many Libertarians support the party's candidates because of their view of what personal freedom is. "Don't tell me or anyone else what to do, let people worship or have sex with whoever they want."

Obviously that part of party philosophy wouldn't sit well with a lot of Christians who typically vote Republican, even if they agree with mostly everything else. There's a huge segment of the conservative Republican (even "libertarian-minded") faction that would never consider joining the Libertarian Party for that reason.

Can the Libertarian Party be a vehicle for what conservatives want?

Yes, but I have trouble seeing it become a "winning party" without coming to some sort of accommodation with Christians and moral conservatives. Their current predominantly pro-abortion position conflicts with their stand in favor of individual rights.

It's not that there are no pro-life Libertarians. I've met plenty. I've even met several who believe the Libertarian Party is pro-life, or at least neutral. I've asked them to identify any pro-life candidates (in Colorado, which is probably typical of non-Southern states), and they are surprised to find there are none, or very few. I've never spoken to a Libertarian candidate on the ballot in Colorado who is for pro-life government policies (some may say they're "personally pro-life but don't want government involved – others explain how important it is that women have bodily autonomy and how central it is to Libertarianism that they be allowed to abort at any time for any reason).

For me, the obvious path to that kind of outcome would be adoption of a plank to protect the rights of "every human being," including the unborn, thereby setting the party up in *opposition* to abortion as a violation of human rights.

If this connection can be made – a difficult sell with objectivists and many libertarians – then they may end up embracing pro-life positions.

But for now, they stubbornly insist abortion is a "bedroom issue" not a matter of individual rights (because they do not recognize the unborn child as human). Are rape, incest and pedophilia to be considered "bedroom issues" too? Not to be legislated against by the government? Of course not – the rights of one individual not to be harmed have to be weighed against the lesser right of another to seek pleasure.

If the laws should protect everybody, as the Libertarian ideal seems to say, why exclude some human individuals from that protection?

But that's the key question – if Libertarians believe the government should protect the rights of individuals, they have to include all individuals or their ideals are meaningless.

That battle – the debate over whether to support abortion as a right, or prohibit abortion as a violation of rights – is present within the Libertarian Party today. But at present the pro-abortion side holds a pretty substantial edge.

Libertarians also miss another aspect of social conservatism that bears closely upon fiscal conservatism. Much of the budgetary crisis in this country ties in one way or another with a failure of social standards. The breakdown of the family is key.

Most families on welfare are led by single moms. Three quarters of the convicts in the criminal justice system are from single parent households. A growing culture of generational violence and lack of compassion is aided by a breakdown in our value for the worth and sanctity of life. Killing babies if they're inconvenient builds a foundation for amoral utilitarianism in other sectors of society, and the rights of the individual are *never* safe in a utilitarian society.

A reduction in childbirth and the breakdown of the family is complicating care for the elderly, who were traditionally cared for by their family. Expensive institutions have grown up to solve or handle all of these problems – welfare, Social Security, Medicare, Medicaid, prisons, etc.

Nothing exists within a vacuum. If billions of dollars are spent by government to deal with societal problems caused by a reduction in family values and a degradation of family units, then ignoring social issues brings a high budgetary cost!

Switching to Third Parties

But why not just join these third parties, if they're the ones who stand strongest for our values?

Because I'm not convinced that's the best use of our efforts. As I've said, it often takes so much money, time and effort to make a third party viable, when the Republican Party is already there and much of the registered members believe as we do anyway.

I know a lot of people who I deeply respect who insist the GOP is a lost cause. Too corrupt. Too large a tent. A morass. They wanted out. Permanently.

Though I disagree, I can't fault them for how they feel.

I've heard many suggest conservative Republicans should just bolt the Republican Party and become Libertarian. Unless they change their positions on social issues I don't find this a realistic solution (though if that many Republicans switched, it might force the issue).

For that reason I see the socially and fiscally conservative American Constitution Party as a more realistic home for conservatives to take the place of the Republican Party. The ACP platform is very like a stronger version of the Republicans' own, with a few key exceptions.

The party known as America's Party (formerly the American Independent Party – Ambassador Alan Keyes was the AIP candidate for president in 2008) has a platform even closer to the true ideals of the Republican Party, but has a much stronger emphasis on Christian and constitutional principles. They endorse candidates from other parties as a way of incorporating the best of both worlds. It's possible to maintain the benefits of Republican Party organization while adhering to the very firm set of values America's Party requires.

Obviously it's not going to be productive or effective if conservatives split into multiple camps, one socially conservative, others socially progressive. That would deny each the critical mass to really replace one of the major parties.

If things really come to a head, and real conservatives are forced to leave the GOP – or, just as likely, the Republican Party leaves their conservatives out in the cold long enough they have to find another home – things could completely shatter and realign, coalescing into a pattern entirely different from what we have now.

If conservatives left the Republican Party, the GOP would move to the middle, drawing in Democrats who aren't loony left. That would fracture the Democrats. You might have a period where no party was transcendent. Maybe four parties drawing significant vote totals. Constitutionally, it will eventually settle into an equilibrium with only two parties on top. But it might get messy for a while.

In the end, conservatives won't end up in a small party – our ideas are too strong. We won't be the losers. We'll be one of the two parties. Though it's anyone's guess what the larger coalition might be that draws in enough people to sustain a major party.

The Tea Party – Taxed Enough Already!

Early on, when the Tea Party first began to rear its head, I was hoping it would become a third party strong enough to challenge the Republicans. I was tired of Republican compromises, and so were most Tea Party people.

At that time the Tea Party had the energy and critical mass to make the quantum leap to near-major party status.

Instead, it turned its attention toward making changes within the Republican Party structure and backing true conservatives within that party.

Some of this – definitely not all, perhaps not most – was subornation.

They brought a lot of people under the Tea Party banner – so many that it began to resemble a "big tent" itself. And that offered tremendous potential – all those people wanting the GOP to stand up for what it said it believed.

But then again, many of these new recruits had been subconsciously trained, so they brought their "party first" attitudes with them.

It's not wrong to think that it's wisest to use an already existing organization – one, coincidentally, that has a party platform identical to the one you're trying to push. The Republican Party was an already-built vehicle for change. The Tea Party just had to take the steering wheel and drive it right.

It's been an experiment of mixed results.

The Tea Party was still taking shape in 2008. Its members were somewhat split during the 2008 presidential primary race, between Fmr. Gov. Mike Huckabee (R-AR) and Congressman Ron Paul (R-TX). Both offered some ideas that were dear to the hearts of Tea Party members. Neither completely fit the bill.

Sen. Fred Thompson (R-TN) might have become a consensus candidate between the Establishment and the Tea Party, but that was too far a gulf to bridge.

In the primary, where most of the attention was already focused on finding "the moderate who can win," the Tea Party got steamrolled by the Establishment.

By 2010, the Tea Party was in charge nationally, and it showed. ABC's November exit polling showed 41% of voters identified themselves as Tea Party (31% said they opposed it). Conservatives – by and large, *real* conservatives – ran, and many of them won. The Congress shifted noticeably to the right, though the staying power of principles in Washington has been sorely tested.

There was a "noise" made, after the election, about how vulnerable key Tea Party nominees for the U.S. Senate were. Some of that was mistakes made by candidates because they were relative newcomers to the glaring lights of the national political field. But there were many successes among Tea Party candidates. More Tea Party candidates for US Senate won than lost, and half of 60 US House seats won by Republicans were won by Tea Party candidates.

There were also failures among moderate, Establishment types. No was no actual trend against the Tea Party.

If anything, top-of-the-ticket Tea Party candidates failed because Republican talking heads labeled them as "extreme" and predicted they would lose, and voters of all stripes trusted that the talking heads were right. Some Establishment people actively worked against Tea Party candidates.

Those talking heads were either ignorant of how to really win elections (they didn't understand politics or they listened to their own "conventional wisdom"), or they were trying to protect the GOP Establishment from totally losing control of the party agenda.

The Tea Party again showed strength in 2012. Tea Party supporters provided momentum for no fewer than five of the six main contenders for the 2012 Republican presidential nomination. But the Establishment started to retrench – worked to successfully convince many conservatives that "Tea Party candidates" were bad bets, and not the way to go.

The Need for More Caffeine

These last three election cycles need to be taken as a lesson for conservatives. We need better vetting for candidates, some of whom had skeletons in their closets no one knew about because newcomers hadn't been around long enough.

It's a difficulty of moving to a citizen government model from the tried and true (but stultifying and pro-Establishment) process of raising people to higher office who've been around a long time and "it's their turn."

More education needs to be done. On the subject of political philosophy, which the Tea Party usually does pretty well. On the subject of communication and messaging, which is "in need of improvement." And on the subject of running campaigns, which any candidate needs, but which can be offset by reliance on experienced campaign staff and volunteers, all of which are generally available to Tea Party candidates.

I believe the Tea Party still has the potential to become a true third party. Perhaps if the GOP once more forces through an Establishment candidate in the 2016 presidential primary, that will be the impetus needed for the Tea Party to separate.

But I also still feel the Tea Party has the power and opportunity to make sure that doesn't happen – to ensure a principled, conservative candidate is nominated for president in 2016. That would be the best of both worlds, having that access to the loyalty of more moderate voters, having the backing of government officials all across the nation who want their party to win, having the benefit of grassroots neighborhood organizations already built and networked.

In 2014 we find the Tea Party wrestling with its identity – struggling to either obey the training which suborned its membership to vote for statist Republicans or to again find its own voice and its own power to remake America, either by taking over the Republican Party for real, or by striking out on its own as a third party.

That next presidential election could be where the Tea Party achieves its goals, one way or another. The ideas of Ronald

Reagan and other conservatives could again be realized by the GOP itself, or the victory of the Establishment could energize and spur principled conservatives to leave the GOP behind.

Whichever choice the Tea Party makes, it needs to be coordinated. We can't have half the membership go one way and half the other.

In the end if the Tea Party can properly execute pressure politics and use its influence to take over and reform the existing GOP structure, that is the clearest and easiest route to power and conservative dominance.

Chapter 8
A Plea To Christian Conservatives

"A private faith that does not act in the face of oppression is no faith at all." – William Wilberforce, British Member of Parliament and Leader of the British Abolitionists

I desperately wish to write a heartfelt personal appeal to Christian conservatives, and to press home a specific application of the message I've been making throughout this book.

I speak primarily to Protestants, because we have become codependently attached to the Republican Party.

But I also aim this partially at Catholics, many of whom are tightly wedded to the Democrat Party because of a feeling of government obligation to the poor. Other Catholics share the conundrum of Protestants who vote Republican because of pro-life issues, and then find themselves disappointed when the GOP doesn't seem to deserve that loyalty.

Christian voters – the so-called "moral majority" – comprise a huge and powerful voting bloc.

Ideally we would use our influence to make society a better place, as Christians did when they adopted children in ancient Greece who had been "exposed" and left to die, or moved a society to ban slavery in Britain and later the United States.

To promote family-friendly policies. To fight corruption.

To do as much as we can to make America a pleasing and respectful country in God's eyes. To call our leaders to take into account the teachings of the Bible, as our Founding Fathers did, in drafting laws to encourage freedom, opportunity, charity, fairness and justice.

To ensure America is a great place to live and raise a family, and that our laws are not in conflict with what God would desire for us.

But Christian conservatives have often been manipulated by fearmongers into voting for the lesser of two evils. Even in circumstances where the lesser man certainly embraced some degree of true evil, generally centered around the subject of abortion.

Evangelical Christians, as with the larger population of Tea Party and liberty-minded people, have been trained – enthralled – to act against their own interests and to support a party and candidates who seek more to *use* them than to listen to them.

We have been taught by the Establishment, with the well-meaning, mostly unconscious complicity of our own religious leaders, to apply relativistic standards in determining which candidates to support. We've been taught to be more afraid of the worst evil, therefore made less guarded toward the lesser evil, which we have often embraced and treated with undue regard, as if he or she will rescue us from the greater evil.

Paul reminds us in Romans 3 that *we should not do evil that good may come.* Some "slanderously" claimed he and his people were doing so, and Paul said if it were true, "Their condemnation is just."

Just what kind of evil could be done that would result in good? God works all things for good, but that's not what Paul was talking about – he specifically *condemned* men who "do evil that good may come."

Surely, isn't he talking about compromises made – committing "little" or "lesser evils" – with the best of intentions, in the expectation that good will come of it? To fight a greater evil?

How more directly and clearly could Paul have condemned "lesser of two evils" thinking?

We Are the Mistress of the GOP

Focus on the Family founder James Dobson once charged that evangelical Christians have become the "mistress" to the Republican Party, recognizing how Christians were brought out when useful for the election and put away again afterward, expected to remain hidden and silent.

Black Democrats experience this same sort of abuse from their party, for the very same reasons as Christians do from the Republican Party.

We're made to feel special at election time. We're talked into being a driving force. Then we're shut away and we don't get anything but scraps, and lip service in return, instead of what was promised.

Dobson had come to recognize the cycle of abuse.

"We know what's best for you – let us run the country, and don't get in the way."

We've brought it upon ourselves – Blacks and Christians alike – through unyielding loyalty to "our" party.

Many will take this as an excuse for Christians to disengage themselves from politics entirely, considering it a dirty business.

It's true, nobody's perfect. The myth of "electing Godly men" is being too charitable, by half. Even many of our religious leaders fall into scandal. But that doesn't mean we and the leaders we vote for can't have a positive influence on politics and society.

I believe it's possible for Christians to participate in such a way to positively influence our political leadership so that our government officials will lead in ways that are less damaging and more respectful of Biblical standards.

Let's find those men and women who respect us and honor God. Then let's vote for them.

I believe, in fact, that it is incumbent upon us to do this.

It's our duty and Biblical mandate to do what we can to improve our broken societies, whether in ancient pagan cultures, in a persecutive country, or in the United States.

At the same time we must prevent ourselves from being entirely suborned and drawn away from what the Bible teaches. We can't be "Republican Christians." And I fear too many of us already are.

Fear Is Not From God

There is perhaps no more famous Psalm than Psalm 23, where David recites, "Yea, though I walk through the valley of the shadow of death, I will fear no evil, for you are with me; Your rod and Your staff, they comfort me."

And that's just the beginning. In Psalm 27, we're reminded, "The Lord is my light and my salvation. Whom shall I fear? The Lord is the strength of my life; Of whom shall I be afraid?" The author of Hebrews reiterates this, recalling the promises of God.

The Prophet Isaiah, in chapter 41, quotes God Himself, saying, "Fear not, for I am with you; Be not dismayed, for I am your God. I will strengthen you. Yes, I will help you, I will uphold you with my righteous right hand."

First Peter 3 reads, "And who is he who will harm you if you become followers of what is good? But even if you should suffer for righteousness' sake, you are blessed. 'And do not be afraid of their threats, nor be troubled...' That when they defame you as evildoers, those who revile your good conduct in Christ may be ashamed."

Psalm 118 says, "The Lord is on my side; I will not fear. What can man do to me?"

Yet many Christians live in fear of every political outcome, and make fear-based decisions about what they must do to better secure their position in our society.

This is a result of our application of "man's wisdom," which seems so much more immediate and compelling in the reality of the present. Man's wisdom – experts and conventional wisdom – has been allowed to drown out the advice offered in the Bible.

Paul's first letter to the Corinthians (1 Corinthians) is replete with denigrations of man's wisdom. "Wise men" consider God's wisdom to be foolishness. Paul makes it clear the opposite is true.

"And my speech and my preaching were not with persuasive words of human wisdom, but in demonstration of the Spirit and of power, that your faith should not be in the wisdom of men but in the power of God." (1 Cor. 2:4-5)

Men should trust in God's wisdom – the wisdom imparted to us through the Bible. We are not to trust in the "persuasive words" of men's wisdom.

And man's wisdom *is* persuasive, isn't it? How many of us have not set aside at least some of what we are told to trust by faith in order to concede some point to man's logic and reason? "Surely He didn't mean that! That would be crazy, right?"

How else is it that we have been so trained to act against our own interests? And worse, against the teachings of God?

God gave us rationality and intellect in order to *understand* His teachings, not to supersede or supplant them. So we could take from scripture what He intended, and discern truth from falsehood.

We are to stand up for righteousness – for policies and people *honoring* to God – not to compromise on moral issues to save some vestige of what is valued by the mind of man. Not to save "what's ours." We need to protect what is *His*.

These reminders are *absolutely not* a call to withdraw from society and politics. Quite the opposite. It is ever more important for us to make a positive impact on society through our actions and opportunities.

And what is more of an opportunity than our coveted ability to vote in this American society?

So why are we wasting our votes by voting against *our values instead of voting intentionally to defend them?*

People are flawed and fallible. Even when we vote for someone who pledges to uphold God's standards we cannot count on that person's faithfulness or continued commitments.

We should not hold trust in that person, or hold them up as an icon.

But at least we can know we voted for a flawed person who nevertheless pledged to honor God, instead of telling us they intend immoral policies – *evil* policies, even! – yet they expect us to support them anyway because man's wisdom or fear tells us to.

Religious Freedom

Many Christians' fear-based voting is very personal. Perhaps concerned not just with their own freedom to worship, but that of every other American Christian.

And I do not deny that we have seen some worrying challenges to these freedoms.

But do such assaults upon our freedoms justify fear-based voting when such reactions undermine us on moral ground even as they may temporarily secure our freedom to worship?

When did we decide turning a deaf ear to the lives of a million unborn children every year was justified in the interest of preserving "religious freedom?"

What good is that freedom if we don't exercise it?!

Focus on the Family president Jim Daly once met some Christians in Communist China and asked what they would wish for Christians in America. They answered, "Greater persecution," because it is that persecution which has made believers in China and half the world much stronger Christians than we are here in the cozy, casual United States.

I mean, having an HOA or a local government tell us we can't have churchgoers parked on the street is a far cry from having to slip through a basement window in the dark of night to study an illegally smuggled Bible.

We have been at ease in Zion, not having our faith greatly tested, and we've grown weak. Our connection to Biblical teachings and the supernatural reality of good and evil is detached. Being threatened with death, as Christians are in Syria and Iraq, or Egypt, has a way of separating the wheat from the chaff.

Those who remain steadfast are serious Christians. Many are in mortal peril for their beliefs. Some have their earthly existence come to an end. But we are taught, without deception, that what we know here on Earth is just the beginning of our existence.

Going back to Psalm 118, "What can man do to me?"

Matthew, in Chapter 10, writes, "Do not fear those who kill the body but cannot kill the soul. But rather fear Him who is able to destroy both soul and body in hell."

It's a reminder that we are all immortal – the faithful are meant to dwell with God in glory.

Christians' lives are not to be finished here on this Earth. Not on *this* corrupted version, anyway.

In his book, *Heaven*, Randy Alcorn suggests that maybe many Christians don't believe in their hearts that Heaven is real, or even the afterlife. The promise of Heaven doesn't seem real when we are invested in and distracted by our mundane existence on this Earth. It seems plenty exciting in the moment, and who wants to let all this go?

But we are assured of the reality of Heaven in the Bible.

Christians cannot let fear of "the bogeyman" prod us into voting for those who oppose much of what we believe. Fear is not an excuse in God's eyes. He assures us that we are His, and His hand is on our shoulder, no matter what dangers or turmoil we face.

The *Lesser* of Two *Real* Evils?

Some things you may not like are *not* evil.

You may think a tax on food is evil. It's not. It may be detrimental to some people – it may cause a hardship – but it's a policy choice a reasonable, well-meaning legislator may support.

You may think a minimum wage of only $8/hr is evil. It's not. Again, it may cause some hardship, but it's a legitimate policy choice of government.

It may be that – taken together – a combination of *many* things that cause small hardship creates a greater hardship. That's oppression. Our Founders claimed a combination of such "outrages" constituted an inexcusable regime of tyranny, and that's how the first Tea Party came about.

Oppression may rate as evil. But again it's debatable. Is a tax burden greater than 10% evil? Or does it have to be 30% or more?

There is *real* evil in the world. We know the Holocaust was evil. Many say war is evil. What about a war to prevent the Holocaust?

Where do you draw the line? Some things are more clear than others.

I think most Christians would agree we should not do what is evil. We should not *participate* in evil. Disagreements crop up when you start talking about "the lesser of two evils."

Since we're Christians, isn't it reasonable that a person on each side of that debate should be able to present a Biblical, scriptural defense of their position?

In ancient Palestine, Jews lived under constant persecution and in close proximity to a degrading, hedonistic, Baal-worshipping, child-sacrificing dominant Canaanite society.

Did the Bible ever recommend the Israelites should vote for the "less evil of two Philistines?!"

The obvious fact is that Jews had no power to vote for or against the evil leaders of the surrounding culture. But *if they had* there is no evidence that God would have advised them to deal with the Canaanites in order to get better terms, or less persecution. To do so would have required a diminution of their holiness and probably a partial acceptance of the worship practices and hedonism of the culture.

Not that many Jews didn't compromise and accommodate anyway. God laments in the early books of the Bible the fact that so many of His people "went over" to paganism because it was easier and more comfortable.

But the Bible does not counsel that Israelites should have found accommodation with their enemies – to support or encourage a "lesser Philistine."

How many, I wonder, did so gradually. Compromising just a little at each time, for the most innocent of reasons or least desires.

Put in a more modern context, would you vote for a candidate who pledged, "I promise I will advocate for the killing of no more than three innocent Jews!?" Would you tell your friends, "He's nearly a Nazi, but at least he won't kill as many Jews. C'mon, let's vote for him!"?

You're horrified, right? You'd *never* support someone like that!

But what if he were the "lesser of two evils?" What if his opponent promised wholesale slaughter, and the "lesser killer" was the more moderate candidate?

This, sadly, is the choice many Christians face on ballots today – not killing Jews, but killing babies. More tragic, still, many pro-lifers have been trained – taught by our pro-life leaders – to vote for whichever candidate supports killing fewer innocent people.

Sadly, because we've accepted the moral compromise for the lesser of two evils, we've "bought in" to some of the evil.

It has to stop. We have to stop it – to *resolve* not to allow this to continue.

There has to be a standard beyond which Christians will not go.

But first we have to understand some of the reasoning that has led us to these compromises in the first place.

Splitting the Difference Today

So where should a Christian come down on a candidate whose position "splits the difference" on abortion? What if that candidate "opposes abortion," say, but supports federal funding for the destruction of human embryos for research purposes (how is that *not* cannibalistic and "creepy evil")?

Or a candidate thinks the killing of innocent children is mostly wrong, but okay in some circumstances?

That really depends on where *God* draws *His* line, as to what is truly evil.

Even Christian denominations differ on what they consider evil. Envy? Possibly. Adultery or contempt for God? Sure – and worth considering in your voting decisions.

But what stands at the top of everybody's list for evil? Slavery? Once upon a time. Murder of the innocent? I would certainly think so.

But in the past Christian conservatives were willing – using "lesser of two evils" thinking – to support Republican candidates who supported abortion in cases of rape or incest, or even who supported abortion completely, except for perhaps being "opposed to partial birth abortion."

Sadly, pro-life groups and online news sources were often complicit, by endorsing these candidates as "pro-life" despite their support for some *or most* abortions.

Remember Sen. Scott Brown (R-MA)? In the 2010 election after Sen. Edward Kennedy (D-MA) passed away, Brown was hailed as "one of us" by Christian and pro-life groups. But, except for supporting some limited discouragements to abortion, he often stood against Christians or the Republican Party platform while in office.

Christians got him there! And that's how he repays us?

Brown's election really did very little to aid the pro-life cause. He supported "freedom of conscience" laws that allow medical providers to refuse to perform abortions, opposed partial birth abortion and supported parental notification laws. But, you will note, these are *the least* any candidate could do for the pro-life cause. There are *Democrats* who hold similar positions!

Christians have been taught (trained) to support these lesser of two evils candidates because of what little good we can get out of them, while learning to accept and overlook the "evil" they do support.

It's a lie that's causing conservatives – and Christians – to unintentionally vote against their interests. The only people who really benefit are the Republican Establishment.

But Brown was promoted by so many Christians and conservatives based on the myth that it's always better to have more members of a preferred party in office, regardless of their views on the issues.

Next election, we were told by Christians and pro-lifers to support Brown against his opponent, who "would be much worse." But this blind support precludes any opportunity to get a real conservative, or a real pro-life candidate, into that seat.

Brown lost, in 2012. Now in 2014 he's running for the US Senate in New Hampshire (he moved). He now says he opposes federal funding of abortions. But while he was a US senator he apparently voted to allow abortions on military bases and to provide federal funding for Planned Parenthood.

When the New Hampshire Republican Party adopted a platform plank affirming the Personhood of the unborn child, the media asked Brown for his reaction. His office issued a statement saying Brown "is pro-choice and will protect a woman's right to choose."

But you can be sure Christians will be tasked once more to prop up his candidacy because "he's better than the other guy (girl)." There are only so many US senators who are as progressive/liberal as Brown is, and fewer of those happen to be Republicans. Nevertheless...

We end up being "the mistress" again – the GOP gets what it wants, which isn't either a conservative or a pro-lifer. But we're expected to be satisfied with what we Christians get, which is very little.

We're expected – and urged by our own leaders – to work hard to keep Brown and others like him in office, "because the alternative would be worse!"

Settling for second best is second nature for us now. It's how we've been trained.

As I've been explaining, this is a self-defeating habit. Each time we give in and accept the lesser of two evils we lose more influence over the process.

These compromises may work in our favor in *limited* ways on the short term, but it actually works against us in *most* ways even in the short term. Worse, it denies *any* long term strategy for success, because we cannot work for anyone who *meets* our standards while also supporting the lesser of two evils candidate.

If a Democrat were in that office – someone opposed to our views in every way – there would be no question that Christians would be working to replace him or her with a pro-life candidate.

We're missing opportunities to work for people who we agree with! We *could* be working to get *them* into office instead.

We're told to fear the negative impact of electing Democrats, but often the Republican isn't much better on the short term, for the advancement of a pro-life or pro-family agenda, and in the long term it can be a *disaster* to any transformational strategy!

What Are We Told We'll Gain?

Critics will say, "Yes, yes, the lesser of two evils and all that. You don't realize how much is at stake, and what we'll gain if this guy wins!"

There are two main reasons we're told by religious leaders and/or Establishment mouthpieces that Christians will benefit by electing moderate Republicans.

The first is "majority status," which we've already discussed and dismissed as worthless or worse (absent a majority of strong pro-family conservatives within the caucus).

We're repeatedly told that a strong Republican minority will hold the line against the Democrats' abortion-on-demand platform. A Republican majority in either house will be better.

And if we're *really* good, and get Republicans in control of both houses and the White House... *That's when the glory days will happen* for Christian conservatives, and the Republicans can really do something to stop abortion.

But wait... *Didn't we have that?*

Dr. James Dobson, founder of Focus on the Family, complained, "We had the Triple Crown!" He was referring to the six years between 2000 and 2006. "We had the White House, the House and the Senate. And the Republicans sat there for six years and did almost nothing!"

Keep in mind that the Establishment are not ideologues – they don't care about the platform. They care only about

127

victory – winning. When a political party is concerned with winning and manipulating the electorate, they don't want to solve problems or completely keep their campaign promises, because then they wouldn't be able to use those election issues in the next election! They'd have to come up with new heartstrings to pluck, and it's so much easier to just use the same ones over and over.

We are the mistress. We were lied to – promised things that were never intended.

It's going to happen again unless we change our habits and take charge of things.

Conservative Judges

The other reason given, which often seems to work better in manipulating Christians, is "conservative judges." If we elect Republicans, we'll get more conservatives and pro-lifers on the court and they will overturn Roe v. Wade!

These supposed conservatives are always contrasted with the "activist judges" Democrats will appoint.

But we have a problem with quality control here too. *We always have.*

Reagan appointed Justice Sandra Day O'Connor, who promised him to his face that she was pro-life. But she neglected to mention she was only "personally pro-life" but professionally pro-choice (a gambit many Republican politicians will play with *you*, if you let them).

Both of George W. Bush's appointees, Chief Justice John Roberts and Justice Samuel Alito, told Congress they believed Roe v. Wade was "settled law." So it's unclear if we can count on their vote to overturn.

Alito had even ruled, previously, that a ban on partial birth abortion was unconstitutional!

Chief Justice Roberts also ruled that Obamacare was legal, because it was a tax. Never mind the many constitutional objections to its massive violations of the Tenth Amendment.

I don't buy the "clever dog" excuse – that Roberts ruled it a tax so it could be destroyed somehow. Even before he was nominated, Roberts' conservative credentials were suspect. The Obamacare ruling only confirmed that.

Many Christians uphold Justices Thomas and Scalia as legitimately pro-life, but how many Christians know *neither one believes there is a Right to Life for anyone before birth?!* Scalia himself said rights are only for "walking around people" (his words).

The "landmark" Gonzales v. Carhart ruling of 2007 was hailed as the most pro-life ruling in decades, supposedly banning partial birth abortion. A closer analysis will show that not to be the case.

The most conservative part of the ruling was the Scalia-Thomas concurring opinion, saying simply that Roe v. Wade was incorrectly decided. The *second*-worst part of the ruling was the justices decided that some partial birth abortions were banned, but others (they provided instructions in the ruling for how the abortionist could pull the baby partially out of the womb before crushing the skull) were *still perfectly legal!*

The justices *did* encourage doctors to use more "humane" methods to kill late-term babies. As if serial murderers would be somehow "nicer" if they chloroformed their victims before slashing their throats.

The *worst* part of Gonzales v. Carhart was that it established that abortion for any reason (including as "birth control") was allowed through the full nine months of pregnancy.

They ruled the *only* reason the so-called "Partial Birth Abortion Ban" was *not* unconstitutional was that it did not create a significant obstacle to "the abortion right" (because, as noted, there are other perfectly legal ways to kill a baby immediately before birth).

Gonzales v. Carhart was actually a far more pro-abortion ruling than Roe v. Wade was.

And *these* are the "pro-life justices" we'll get more of if we vote Republican?

Hmm...

Each of the justices has problems. They are not so conservative as we were told.

Some conservative and Christian commentators have even suggested this is a good thing – they say if they were *really* conservative they would be "activist." As if standing up for the Constitution, or the Right to Life, is being "activist." That's rubbish.

Do Christians benefit some from having "more conservative" judges on the Supreme Court?

Yes. We get favorable rulings on some family issues, and on religious freedom issues (the Hobby Lobby decision was a victory, but surely they would go no further than they did, which wasn't a complete victory for freedom of conscience).

Again we face the tradeoff situation. Do we settle for a less-than-principled court justice, who will deliver occasional anti-liberty rulings, pro-abortion rulings, etc., in order to get a handful of conservative opinions?

Or do we recognize, as we have with the political leadership in Washington and elsewhere, that the system is broken and we need to do a complete reform and overhaul?

The Republicans we're electing don't understand the concept of an actual Right to Life for the unborn, so neither do the judges they appoint and approve.

We're *not* gaining what we really want.

We need to reassess. We need to quit doing what we've been doing.

Start over and do it right instead.

In my upcoming book on Personhood, I will establish that none of the current justices believes in a Right to Life for the unborn, and I will propose (as others before me have) we have to start over in appointing justices who will recognize the human rights of the unborn, which naturally must start with electing *politicians* who believe in an actual, Constitutionally protected Right to Life for unborn humans.

Being "As Wise as Serpents"

The #1 most oft-cited Bible verse for political Christians (or so I surmise, from cynical experience) is Matthew 10:16. "I am sending you out like sheep among the wolves. Therefore be as shrewd as snakes and as innocent as doves" (another translation says "as wise as serpents").

That's the verse political Christians pull out when others say we cannot vote for the lesser of two evils.

It's intended to say, "Ahh, but the Bible tells us to be shrewdly wise and sly in our choices, so it's okay for us to vote for a lesser evil to defeat the greater evil. We're being clever."

Yes, too much by half.

I do not think that's what God had in mind. Paul tells us not to do evil that good may come. Back to our extreme logical conclusion test.

Was God telling us to vote for Hitler so the communists don't win?

Given the apparent conflict between "shrewd as snakes" and "that good may come," some discernment is necessary. Look at the scriptures in context. It's the easy way out to use "shrewd as snakes" as a "get out of jail free card."

Does it mean it's okay to vote for the pro-slavery candidate, over the slave-*owning* candidate?

Or does it *more likely* mean lying when the soldier with the sword comes and asks if you've seen the Baby Moses?

Now, a shrewd student of the Bible might say, "Isn't lying still doing evil that good may come?"

But the Bible honors Pharaoh's daughter and the nursemaids, even though they lied by omission in hiding the child, and broke the Pharaoh's law. Instead of following an unjust law, they did what's right.

Rahab is also honored for outright lies to the authorities in Jericho to hide the Hebrew spies. Imagine that – a treasonous prostitute as a hero of the Bible!

What would the Bible say about lying to hide Jews from the Gestapo?

Keep in mind that none of these circumstances involves *participation* in actual evil.

Discernment tells us the Bible seems to be saying, "Don't major in the minors. Participating in evil is evil. Lying for your own benefit is a sin. Lying isn't evil if your intentions are pure and it upholds justice and righteousness *against* evil. Same with pulling a man out of quicksand on the Sabbath."

"Exactly my point!!!" the political Christian shouts.

But hold on. Let's test this.

Does voting for the lesser of two evils constitute *participating* in the evil? And does it uphold justice and righteousness?

I know most political Christians are still going to say "no" and "yes," and I bang my head against a wall because of it. But that's how they've been trained. Even by religious leaders they (and probably I) respect.

The religious leaders *themselves* have been trained in Establishment thinking.

My answer is "yes" and "no."

Matthew 10:16 has some strange sentence construction. Why pair "shrewd or wise as serpents" with "innocent as doves?"

I wonder if perhaps it's meant to mean you can be as shrewd as a snake *so long as you remain* as innocent as doves. I.e. so long as both your intentions and actions remain pure.

When you vote for someone, you are *enabling* that person to do what he will. And you know — because he or she has said so — he intends some evil, or you wouldn't consider him the "lesser evil."

So you're *enabling* actual evil, even if it's lesser, be it slavery or abortion or whatever.

Worse, if you campaign for them and pressure friends to vote for them...

Your *intentions* may be pure — it meets *that* test — but supporting and enabling a candidate who intends actual evil (even a lesser evil) does *not* uphold justice and righteousness.

So voting for the lesser of two evils does not qualify as being "wise as serpents."

It qualifies, instead, as doing evil that good may come, which is forbidden.

Sarah Palin & Paul Ryan

In both the 2008 and 2012 elections, neither of the two major parties nominated pro-life candidates for president.

Barack Obama was the overtly pro-abortion candidate — the one who had voted to support abortion even in the fourth trimester (i.e. after birth, following a failed abortion).

But John McCain was not a legitimately pro-life candidate, and never had been. Neither was Mitt Romney. Not unless you mess with the standards for what "pro-life" means.

Both McCain and Romney had spoken in favor of a woman's "right to choose", had supported Roe v. Wade in statements, had always held to a rape/incest exception, and had even favored taxpayer funding of abortions. McCain pretended, during his 2008 campaign, to be 100 percent pro-life, because he knew he had to motivate Christians to vote for him.

He said, wisely, if not honestly, that he believed life began at conception. Yet, he never gave up his position in favor of embryonic stem cell experiments which kill a developing human embryo after conception.

That had always been a pet issue for him – research that killed a developing human being in order to improve the lives of "people who are already alive" (as they say in "the biz").

So, McCain believes life begins at conception, but stubbornly insists it should be okay to kill those lives if it's for a good cause?

Then he forced his running mate, former Gov. Sarah Palin to sign on with him on stem cell research.

Many Christians said they voted for Sarah Palin, not John McCain, hoping somehow that she would make him more conservative and more pro-life.

In 2012, Christians said the same – "I really voted for Paul Ryan. I'm not a big fan of Mitt Romney, but at least Ryan is conservative and can keep him in line."

That's exactly what GOP strategists *wanted* Christians to think – to think that, somehow, Palin would impose her own pro-life views upon John McCain. Or Ryan would impose his more conservative fiscal views on a tax-n-spend statist like Romney.

It doesn't work that way. Vice President Jack Garner served under FDR, and he said the job was "not worth a bucket of warm spit." Garner, who had given up a powerful position as Speaker of the House, added, "Worst damnfool mistake I ever made was letting myself be elected Vice President of the United States... I spent eight long years as Mr. Roosevelt's spare tire."

Dick Cheney was history's most influential Vice President ever, and even he could not have forced his own positions upon the president. That's not the VP's job. And it wouldn't have been Palin's job either. Or Ryan's.

Palin's job, during the campaign, was to support everything John McCain said, and act like he was really as conservative as he was pretending to be. She would have had no more leverage if they had won than she did during the campaign.

George H.W. Bush was forced to pledge to be *more* conservative, when he assumed the role as Reagan's running mate. As the price to pay for becoming Vice President, Bush had to pledge to switch from being pro-choice to being pro-life.

No vice president, and certainly no running mate, has ever been able to significantly influence a candidate on major policy aims. It's always the other way around. If they weren't willing to make excuses for the guy at the top of the ticket in order to draw in votes, they would never have been chosen.

The Most Important Issue of Our Day

What does God *most* want His people to care about in society, outside of our worship for Him?

I know a lot of Christians who think God wants us to care for the poor and suffering... And I certainly agree.

But I believe "caring for the poor and suffering" is *our* job – as individual Christians, and as churches – not government. Charity instead of welfare.

Do you think God was more concerned about the Pharaoh's economy than the enslavement of His people?

God is most offended by moral evil, not temporary suffering. We are told, for instance, to "rescue those being led away to death; hold back those staggering toward slaughter." (Proverbs 24)

Surely, that means spreading the Gospel. But can't it also be interpreted as a mandate against behaviors which work to destroy people?

Maybe that means opposition to drug use. Maybe that means keeping families together.

Whatever it means, I'm a lot more certain it means opposing the killing of unborn children. In ancient Greece and Rome it meant opposing the "exposing" of unwanted children (leaving them on the road to die unfed and unclothed). Many of whom were adopted by Christians instead (just as many Christians today are willing to adopt orphans and/or children born to parents who were considering abortion).

William Wilberforce knew slavery was among those moral imperatives he was called to do something about – it needed to be his mission in life. He knew that his society was being eaten away from the inside because of the corruption that accompanied that well-entrenched institution.

Politicians in the 1800s had many very important things to consider – taxes, tariffs, public works – but how did those things really compare to where someone stood on the issue of slavery as far as what we know about them today or how Christians would have been expected to think about them then?

What was ultimately the most important issue of their age? Taxes or slavery?

What is ultimately the most important issue of *our* age?

More than 50 million unborn children have died from surgical abortion in the United States since the first states began to decriminalize abortion in 1967.

According to the pro-abortion Guttmacher Institute, more than 1 million die each year. More human beings are aborted every day than died at the World Trade Center on 9/11.

Unknown more millions of little human individuals have been first conceived and then starved inside their mothers' wombs as the result of hormonal birth control.

Most Christians have no idea their birth control may be killing their kids.

Even Christian ministries are waking up to this for the first time and are slowly beginning to react.

A politician's position on taxes is important. On spending policy. On states' rights. On welfare. On military strength. On relations with other countries.

It continues to astonish me when Christians vote on the basis of other issues, subordinating a candidate's opinion on abortion – on which kids to kill in the womb – to a number of other issues that seem more important to them at the moment.

Some Christian Republicans have come to believe other issues – jobs, the economy, national prestige – override beliefs on abortion. They especially prefer fiscal issues because they unite conservative Christians with a powerful alliance of people on the moderate-to-conservative Republican/Libertarian axis.

I've had Christians tell me, "Yes, ending abortion is important – I'm pro-life. But our country's in a lot of trouble. We need to deal with the important stuff right now, and we'll come back and end abortion later, after the crisis is past."

"Let's work on the important stuff first."

Would they have said the same in the face of slavery?

Republican officials all over the country tell legislators and candidates to "avoid divisive social issues" so they can sidestep the nasty infighting within the party that results.

This not only reflects a wrongheaded assumption that Republicans have to take moderate positions to win. It also misses the well-established political maxim that motivating and mobilizing your base is the best way to win elections, and the "abortion as human rights violation" debate as a potentially transforming national issue, like slavery.

But I believe it also rejects what should be a Christian belief in "gateway issues" – issues of great moral importance which should be considered prerequisites for Christian support.

What if Stephen Douglas had been the "fiscally conservative" candidate again Lincoln? Would it have been right for anti-slavery voters to put their primary issue aside to choose the fiscally conservative candidate? Or should they (and *would* they) have chosen the overriding moral issue over fiscal and other considerations?

Back then, Christians might well have applied a "gateway issue" standard to slavery – they could support candidates who opposed slavery (all slavery – not just shifting it to the south, which was the 1850s equivalent of modern abortion compromise), and could have applied degrees of grace on other issues.

I believe an increasing number of Christians *did* use that standard in the 1840s and 50s. That's how the anti-slavery Free Soil and Republican parties grew to become strong third parties, and how large numbers of Whig and Democrat voters became associated together instead in the Republican Party – former political opponents joining together to end slavery above other considerations.

Yes, there will always be abortion, just as there will always be slavery. It's a question of whether our government abhors it, and prosecutes it when discovered... or *condones* it instead.

Who's Our Savior?

Pro-lifers have long believed that "salvation" on abortion and other "Christian issues" rested in the hands of the Republican Party. This is partly an outgrowth of the fact that evangelical Christians have, increasingly since 1980, seen the GOP and Republican candidates as "our savior."

This works against Christians because, obviously, the Republican Party is a false god.

It has even worked against the anti-abortion movement by politicizing the pro-life message, causing many Christians who self-identify with a more progressive political posture – favoring care of the poor – to reject the pro-life movement as tainted by political motivations, or worse, a way to keep women or the poor down.

Independents and Democrats, also, have rejected pro-life arguments out of hand, because they assume the Right to Life is either a Republican issue, or a religious issue (independents being as confused as evangelical Christians as to whether there is any distinction between Republicans and Christians).

Ironically, it was mostly Catholic Democrats, not Republicans, who fought the first efforts to legalize abortion. And it was Republican governors, such as John Love in Colorado, and Ronald Reagan in California, who signed the first laws allowing abortion in "special" cases (i.e. rape, incest, the life of the mother). Claims of rape skyrocketed, immediately demonstrating abuse of the law.

Reagan later said he signed it against his better judgment, only because the dozens of Protestant and Catholic religious leaders he asked for moral guidance either said they didn't know, or urged him to sign it for reasons of "compassion" toward rape victims! In retrospect Reagan considered it the biggest mistake he'd ever made.

True, it was the Republican Party, led by Reagan, that took the re-energized pro-life movement under its wing, nurtured it, and gave it some of its early rallying cries and even successes (such as the Hyde Amendment, which despite being compromised with exceptions, was a political success pro-lifers could hold on to for inspiration).

It is also true that, to the extent they can be called pro-life, all of the nominally pro-life justices on the current U.S. Supreme Court have been appointed by Republicans. One of the dissenting opinions in Roe v. Wade was written by Republican

William Rehnquist, though the other was Kennedy-appointee Byron White. Five of the seven justices who supported the Roe v. Wade majority opinion were Republican appointees.

But isn't the abolition of abortion an issue that deserves to be non-partisan – shared by both parties? I believe this can (and will) happen at some point. But not until the issue has been elevated above partisan politics.

But the idealization of party is only part of the problem – the lesser portion.

Many Christians in 1930s Germany came to see Adolf Hitler as their defender against Godless communism – essentially as their "Savior."

I see disturbing trends in United States politics in that direction.

Some Democrats – especially Blacks – saw Barack Obama as a Savior. He even relished the role, and played upon it. He never, that I have seen, humbly asked people to refrain.

But I watched Republican Christians – many of them my friends – regard Mitt Romney with a sense of near worship. He *had* to win, because if he didn't everything Christians cared about would go to Hell.

Romney was to be our *Savior!*

We are not to replace God with man. That is idolatry. We are to trust that we are in the hands of Jesus. That He will care for us, even in a world that has turned against us, even if things get much worse.

Who is our Savior to be today? Or in 2016? A Holy Jesus? Or Romney? Or Rand Paul? Or Chris Christie? Or Ted Cruz? Or Ben Carson?

The Pro-Life Personhood Strategy

So, if we are to avoid embracing moral evil and compromised principle, in choosing our candidates, but still have grace for differences on matters of policy, where do we draw that line?

I believe Christians can accept differences of opinion on many different political issues, so long as they hold firm on the "gateway issues" – if a candidate doesn't meet the standard on those, they don't get past the gate, no matter how much we might agree on other issues.

I am convinced that opposition to the killing of even one innocent unborn child must be that standard for every pro-life voter, no matter what our choices at the ballot box.

The final chapter in this book will offer a preview of my upcoming book, *Persons Not Property*, wherein I will discuss the transformational promise of the Personhood strategy for ending abortion in America.

I will go into it only briefly now.

Ronald Reagan wrote Personhood – in the form of the Human Life Amendment – into the Republican Party platform in 1980. That platform item has not substantially changed since then.

Personhood is the concept that unborn children – every single one, from the moment of their creation as individuals – deserve the right, as human beings, to government's protection of their Right to Life as protected by the 14th Amendment, as well as higher natural laws.

It is not merely a religious view.

The drafters of the Roe v. Wade decision themselves wrote Personhood into the text of the ruling. "We need not resolve the difficult question of when life begins... If this [the State of Texas'] suggestion of personhood is established, the appellant's [pro-abortion] case collapses, for the fetus' right to life is then guaranteed by the 14th Amendment."

Science contains nothing to refute, and *much to recommend*, the inclusion of even single-celled human beings as "one of us." Every decade technology comes closer to solving the question – if there ever was one – of "when life begins."

The media and abortion advocates have distorted Personhood to make it sound like it would ban "contraceptives," which is outright untrue.

First off, it would probably not ban *anything*. Lethal poisons like the rat poison coumadin remain legal to sell – you just can't use them to kill someone, or else you'll be prosecuted for murder.

Secondly, a "contraceptive" is generally held to prevent conception of a human child. Whereas Personhood, as a legal concept, cannot come into force until *after* a human child exists. So unless someone has other legal or philosophical objections, Personhood supporters have no problem with true contraceptives.

Strict Catholics oppose any form of birth control beyond "natural family planning" for a number of very good theological reasons. I'll mention more on that in the final chapter, but this argument is *entirely* separate from the Personhood debate.

The "common forms of birth control" often referred to in campaign ads and news stories related to Personhood are actually abortifacients – chemicals designed to poison and kill the conceived child, or make it impossible for the conceived child to implant in the uterus and begin feeding (i.e. the conceived child is starved). Even though the more potent of these are often called "emergency contraceptives" by doctors, these pills are not "contraceptives" any more than Tylenol with Codeine is merely Tylenol (it's a narcotic).

There are other horror scenarios bandied about wildly. Some will claim that women will be investigated for miscarriages, which is patently ridiculous. You only have to look to the situation before 1967 to get an idea how district attorneys and law enforcement officers might handle such things. They didn't! Not unless there was clear evidence that a woman was trying to intentionally harm her child.

The bottom line is don't believe just anything you might hear about "what Personhood might do" – have the intellectual honesty to give a fair hearing to proponents who can provide answers to these fantastic lies.

So, by adopting a Personhood standard, candidates, politicians and voters are essentially saying they will oppose the killing of an unborn human child for *any* reason, whether performed by medical staff or by means of a pill – opposing both chemical and surgical abortion.

It's the *only* position consistent with an actual Right to Life.

Many will ask about "life of the mother" exceptions – why not allow abortion to be performed to save the life of the mother? In actuality, there *need never be* a "life of the mother" exception to enable a doctor to perform lifesaving work on the mother. The doctor, by his/her Hippocratic Oath, should seek to "do no harm" and should treat *both* the mother and her child as patients, not *trying* to kill either one.

As any doctor would tell you, it's not always possible to save every patient – some will die because their body just doesn't have the ability to keep living. If a pregnancy isn't far enough advanced for there to be a chance of survival, the doctor can still *attempt* to save the baby's life (even though success is almost impossible) while also trying to save the mother. The prognosis for the mother does not improve if the baby is intentionally killed (i.e. abortion) – the result for the mother would be the same, whether the doctor tries to kill the baby or tries to save the baby.

More and more candidates are switching to a 100% pro-life position, with no exceptions. That's largely because the pro-life community at large has increasingly embraced the Personhood position, opposing abortion in all cases.

What's more, several Personhood amendment efforts across the country, as well as the very public Hobby Lobby case and Supreme Court decision, have educated the general public more extensively about "chemical abortion" – the abortifacient pills that can take a baby's life which are those Hobby Lobby refused to pay for in their health plans.

This enlightening discussion about birth control has never happened in this country before, even among most Christians, and so it's having far reaching ramifications now, in that people are starting to realize some forms of birth control could be killing their kids.

All these things are combining to make "pro-lifers" more pro-life than ever before. Sincere pro-lifers who once considered birth control irrelevant are taking another look and realizing that to protect all unborn children they also need to oppose abortion pills.

I believe Christians are never called to support people who believe it's okay to kill even "some" children. I believe those Christian leaders who make excuses for these candidates are wrong.

Any standard but Personhood allows candidates to take one pro-life step at a time, or even just to leave it at lip service. A politician is slow to get anything done, and normally only does what he politically must. If allowed, they will use major issues as election platforms in order to get elected, and won't really act to accomplish anything. We can't allow this.

Candidates who boastfully bear these labels of "pro-life with exceptions" need to be shown up for what they really are – pro-abortion with exceptions. Pro-lifers should not be supporting them, and giving our honored names to support their pro-abortion cause, even if they are "better than the other guy."

If abortion is murder then these candidates are "in favor of murder *in some limited cases.*"

Think about that!

If that were really on their campaign literature, would you still support them?

But because they use euphemisms, and we allow them to get away with it, this compromise has continued.

Through "exception loopholes," the Republican Party ironically became a channel for undermining a culture of life in favor of a permissive abortion culture. Republicans have "earned" pro-life votes without actually promising much, and rarely accomplishing much for the pro-life cause even after being elected.

Remember Dr. Dobson's remark about the "Triple Crown" – Republicans had control of both the Executive and Legislative branches of government. They had all the power, and still did nothing significant to put a stop to abortion. The "fake" Partial Birth Abortion Ban doesn't count, as explained earlier, since it was written without the power to stop any abortions. It was political show, as are many Republican statements against abortion.

Prominent pro-life leaders will disagree. National Right to Life, and many of its affiliates, still campaign on behalf of candidates like Scott Brown who support some abortion. The webnews service LifeNews.com also aggressively opposes Personhood and routinely provides "cover" for Republican candidates with pro-abortion attitudes by labeling candidates like Mitt Romney and John McCain "pro-life" when they support some abortion and certainly don't qualify under the criteria we've discussed here in this book.

Remember, also, that candidates train their supporters. In 2010, the fact that most major candidates for higher office in Colorado supported Personhood brought a lot more Republican voters to adopt Personhood as their personal standard.

I'm concerned that the lack of support from some key 2014 Republican nominees in Colorado may be a stumbling block, and will lead some conservatives and even Christians to reject the Personhood standard.

There will be candidates in many primaries who will take pro-Personhood positions. Candidates should never have excuse to feel like Personhood is a "third rail" for their candidacies.

Their pro-Personhood candidacy becomes a selling point for the Personhood concept.

Therefore, it's important to support Personhood candidates, wherever they are, even if they're not in your district. As I've advertised, I believe Personhood is the 21st Century's equivalent of the anti-slavery abolitionist campaigns of the 1800s.

Wouldn't abolishing the institution of abortion be a proper testimony and an appropriate use of our influence as Christians upon our society?

Chapter 9
Let's Win Instead of Compromising!

"'Carter could beat Reagan more easily than he could Bush or Baker,' Mr. Lewis says, 'A moderate Republican would appeal to moderate Democrats, while upper-income Republicans might defect from Reagan to the Democrats. Ford is, of course, the strongest in the polls against Carter.'" – I.A. Lewis, director of the Los Angeles Times Poll, as quoted in the Christian Science Monitor, March 5, 1980

The GOP Establishment tells Republicans we have to compromise, or else we'll lose.

Republicans have to avoid those dreaded, controversial social issues, or else we'll lose.

Republicans have to moderate their tone and not be "ideologues" (like Reagan?) on major spending and entitlements issues...

Or else we'll lose.

Republicans have to, in fact, remain quiet about most of our platform issues, they say, because the public will think our candidates are crazy, and it's much better if we just sound like more reasonable versions of the Democrats – spend lots, just not as much, grow government programs, just not as fast...

Or else we'll lose.

The GOP in some states – California, New York, Massachusetts, to name just a few – have been using this approach for decades, *and they still lose!*

What's more, outside of particular "red districts," or outside of the South, I've rarely seen Democrats try to simply seem like more reasonable versions of Republicans. No, they push their ideology at every election. They can't have candidates offending their special interest constituencies in the trade unions, the abortion lobby, the trial lawyer associations and various racial and lifestyle pressure groups. They have a checklist, and if you don't publicly espouse every view on the checklist, they "welcome you to end your candidacy" or they put up a more progressive candidate against you in the primary so you can't win.

Democrats have their own voter base trained as well or better than the Republican Establishment has trained theirs. All they have to do is make a false accusation of racism or woman hating, and their activist base covers their eyes and ears and run away.

But in the eyes of the media Democrats are never "extremists" for not compromising their views.

Republicans regularly compromise, and yet we *are* "extremists!"

What are we afraid of? Have we convinced ourselves our ideas really *are* extreme? We should know better.

We should be shouting our values from the rooftops.

We know these ideas work. Let's let others in on the secret!

The Republican Party – the *real* party, not the Establishment – doesn't need to go to that extreme to ensure purity. Republicans are, by their nature, proponents of choices and opponents of coercion. I don't think such behavior would be tolerated in most sectors of the GOP.

True ideas, based in common sense, will prove attractive enough to large sectors of the population so as to aid with the issue of electability. Such ideas, expressed in a partisan Republican framework, will be even more effective.

What we need to exercise, in choosing our candidates, is improved quality control and better positive training in how to think like a conservative and how to message those ideas.

Some elements of an effective training program are here…

Ronald Reagan & Newt Gingrich

If you ever have to explain to someone why the GOP doesn't have to run moderates to win elections, remember this book and remember who the two most successful Republican leaders of the last 30 years have been – Ronald Reagan and Newt Gingrich.

Former Governor Ronald Reagan tried hard in 1976, and more successfully in 1980, to put forward conservative policies of fiscal conservatism and smaller government as the solution for America's problems. He didn't "run to the center" to pick up the votes of moderates and independents. He forcefully called for real change and presented innovative ideas. He made the argument for how conservative policies could remake America for the better and rescue it from the miserable state the Democrats had left it in.

These weren't new ideas for him – not a poll-generated "rebranding" to make him compete more effectively in the contemporary political environment. In 1964 he had expounded on those same ideas in a speech defending Senator Barry Goldwater's bid for the presidency. That speech, known as "A Time for Choosing" on YouTube, remains one of the most simple, most powerful explanations of conservative policy ever produced.

Reagan was the most "extreme" nominee for president the Republicans had ever put forward. Goldwater was close, but Reagan took most of Goldwater's fiscal and foreign policy ideas and married them to a social conservatism that included support for a Human Life Amendment, which in modern language equates to Personhood protections for the unborn child from conception on.

Reagan made that case, for protecting all human beings at all stages of development under the 14th Amendment, and he *still* won by a landslide, collecting votes from Republicans, moderates, independents and even Democrats!

Ronald Reagan didn't say he could use government smarter, or spend less money using federal policies to solve America's problems. He told Americans straight out that *America's problem* was *the government!* Its excessive spending, its drag upon jobs and free enterprise – its intrusion into every citizens' life.

In 1994, US House Minority Leader Newt Gingrich set up the Contract With America, which outlined several promises for legislation they would pass if a Republican majority were elected to Congress. He promised progress – there would be no "do-nothing Congress" on his watch.

He didn't propose moderate, middle-of-the-road policies. He didn't mumble vague assurances.

No, his plan explained ten policy areas where conservative Republicans had clear differences with Democrats. It showed how those policies were grounded in common sense, and it pointed out how Republican ideas could actually solve America's problems, whereas the methods Democrats were using had failed.

Gingrich was rewarded with election victories – 54 House seats and 9 Senate seats – that placed Republicans in control of both chambers. It was a brilliant mandate, showing Americans wanted government to try these ideas.

The energized new House majority passed most of these measures, though not all made it through the Senate (some measures required a supermajority, which Republicans did not have) and few made it past President Bill Clinton despite the clear voice of the people.

Some critics called it a failure because the proposals didn't all make it into law.

No! It was a success because it showed the strength of conservative ideas in the public mind, if properly messaged, and the public's confidence that such measures would be for the betterment of society.

It also proved that a legislative body could hold to its promises, and it provided people with hope that conservative leadership could bring progress out of gridlock toward a better America.

Reagan and Gingrich did not propose lesser evils or centrist ideas as a way to pick up votes. They both proposed real, dramatic, and most importantly conservative changes to government policy.

And *they did not lose* – both achieved remarkable victories over the tired, expensive, bankrupt ideas which were all that the Democrats had in their toolkit.

Gotta Run Moderates!

But the success of Gingrich's Contract With America is lost on today's GOP Establishment.

What if, in 1980, conservatives had said, "Ronald Reagan sure is my first choice for president. I just love his ability to communicate, and the solidity of his principles. But if we intend to win this election against that awful Jimmy Carter we conservatives have to rally around *George H. W. Bush – the moderate who can win!"*

Compared to those who came before him – even many since – Reagan was a hyper-conservative. Yet he won more votes in November than H.W. ever could have.

Republicans have made the mistake of supporting moderates for congress and president "because they can win!"

I can guarantee you what we've been doing isn't working. That's why we don't control both houses of Congress.

As I've already shown, running moderates is a bad bet if you want to win elections. It has as many handicaps as advantages, if not more.

The GOP has been serving up people increasingly toward the middle, thinking moderates will vote for Republicans.

In my experience many voters who consider themselves moderate will vote consistently for one side of the political spectrum or the other – they don't flip back and forth, because their views pretty much remain predominantly on one side or the other. Perhaps remaining independent from a party structure gives them some form of pride, but they do have established ideas on government and vote to support them.

For that reason, those voters who typically vote Republican are less likely to defect to the other party when a candidate moves to take a more conservative position *unless* they are actively urged to by persuasive Republican voices who opt to support the Democrat instead (i.e. Establishment turncoats).

Other "moderates" are not motivated primarily by principle, though some may try to elevate "centrism" to principle status. A voter who really is "moderate" is often simply too uninformed to have developed an opinion on political philosophy. Their idea of "political philosophy" is to keep either side from winning.

Young "moderates" may vote Democrat because they think all their friends are moderate, and their friends vote Democrat, so... "Extremism," to them, is deviation from the norm, and "the norm" for them is the opinions of outspoken progressive youth.

These voters will often prefer a Democrat because Democrat candidates paint themselves as moderates, even though they're not, and the public believes them. GOP candidates – many of them these days – really are moderates, but nobody believes them! That's the media bias manifesting itself against us.

Some moderates are more comfortable with compromise and splitting the difference – it's part of their philosophy, such as it is, so some may be willing to "compromise" and accept a conservative. Others wouldn't accept a conservative in any case, because they are really progressives at heart and will always work against conservative values.

So there's not much ground to be made up, from either the "independent" voters who *have* a political philosophy, or from the so-called "low information" voters who typically vote Democrat because they don't know any better. You're going to have to sound an *awfully* lot like a Democrat to get these voters, and by that point what's the sense in remaining a Republican?

By moving to a more conservative position, though, Republican candidates will pick up more of their own base, which will benefit them *unless* they fail in their messaging and really do come off as a tone-deaf, stereotypical extremist.

They may also pick up votes from dissatisfied, recently engaged voters who are so frustrated they want a serious change (this is where many Tea Party voters came from). Someone looking for "serious change" isn't going to vote for a mush-mouthed Establishment candidate as readily as they will vote for someone who represents a clean break from the status quo.

Even the past decade's voting trend for women who prefer Democrats because of the "womens' rights" canard is a correctable outlier conservatives can take advantage of.

Success in projecting a confident, common sense image versus an "extremist" image has a lot to do with communications training. But it sure helps if the person really believes what they're projecting, because it's hard to sound sincere to a skeptical population when you're not. Especially off the cuff, which is where skeptics will pick up on whether you're just trying to fake it.

GOP leaders think they can get away with this "gotta run moderates" standard because they assume that their Christian base will vote for their candidates, no matter what. They aim to bring as many moderates to the booths as they can, but they have no need to doubt their "right flank" is secure.

But this strategic assumption backfires when the enthusiasm of the base is suppressed, which directly counters their assumptions. Maybe there's not a lot of "sound and fury" from Republicans on the right. We've been shouted down by "party first" folks enough times that most of us just keep our mouths shut. But many don't show up on Election Day when we don't feel it's worth our time.

So why does the Republican National Committee always encourage this strategy if it doesn't work?

Partly because they would rather lose with a moderate, Establishment candidate, than win with anyone from the conservative wing of the party. The 2010 Senate races proved this. The RNC staffers are Establishment operatives and managers. They probably know their jobs are at stake if anyone with new ideas takes office!

We're going the wrong direction, following the wrong strategy. We need to energize the base, and the base has been ignored for so long we're getting angry. Would you have preferred President Rockefeller to President Johnson in 1964? What if Republicans had backed Rockefeller in '64, instead of Goldwater, because Rockefeller was "the guy who could win"?

Goldwater's problem – the reason he didn't win – was less that he was too conservative than that he didn't have a filter and didn't guard his mouth. He made a number of statements that sounded outrageous when quoted back to the American people. He wasn't a "Great Communicator" – he was an ideas guy and policy wonk. A visionary thinker.

But Barry Goldwater built the conservative base of the Republican Party. Without Goldwater, Ronald Reagan would never have made it out of the primaries. The party would have remained a moderate party, and conservatives would have remained out in the cold.

We've got to run conservatives, not moderate-progressive Establishment types.

Otherwise, even when Republicans win, *so do progressives!*

Can't Talk About That!

The strategic recommendations of the Establishment are wrong-headed for a lot of reasons.

One reason why the Establishment mantra has recently been "jobs and the economy" is because they're afraid to talk about anything else!

This ignores the fact that there are very winnable issues to talk about where conservative ideology will prevail. The Establishment isn't interested because they don't *want* to have to talk about conservative ideas.

Candidates are told to avoid talking about abortion because it offends moderates, independents, and even many registered Republicans.

But in order for Republicans to avoid touching off that nerve pro-abortion women have about their "rights," we would have to remain entirely silent on the issue, never bringing it up for fear of offending the pro-abortion members of the Republican "big tent."

That basically means one part of the "big tent" must remain silent about its feelings on rights, allowing them to be quietly violated, and defer to the other members of the "big tent" who get to revel in their own "rights" and speak all they want.

That's what some leaders of the Republican Party have been saying. "We'll be able to win elections if those Christians would just shut up! So long as they still vote for us..."

This is unrealistic. It is disrespectful!

On issues as sensitive as abortion and slavery, it is/was ultimately impossible for one faction to remain in the same party with the other faction. In the 1850s, the constant and perpetual stress of remaining silent on a major moral issue for the "sake of the party" caused a major breakup. The anti-slavery members of the Whigs and Democrats broke ranks, left their parties, and formed a third party.

Likewise, silence will not rescue the GOP. If today's Republican Party continues to pursue the ridiculous "big tent" strategy, papering over the very real stresses of the abortion issue, the very same thing will happen, and the Republican Party will cease to exist, replaced by parties with very clear positions on abortion.

The only way this won't happen is if the issue is liable to go away and present-day anti-abortion voters are willing to let it go. As one of those activists, I can tell you that's not going to happen. Today's pro-life movement is energized, feeling victory is at hand.

The issue isn't going away.

But without taking on the abortion issue head on, or at least having good, reasonable answers for why our candidates hold pro-life views, we allow Democrats to look like *they* are defending peoples' rights, when really it's us. We cede the issue to our opponents, and as columnist Michelle Malkin has warned, we look like we have nothing to answer their charges.

We must *really* hate women, it will seem, if we can't properly explain why we oppose what has been wrongly branded by Democrats as a "womens' rights" issue!

But abortion is just one of the issues the Establishment doesn't want to talk about. It's like they think any issue the Democrats use to attack Republicans is an "unwinnable" issue!

Hogwash! They just don't know how to defend against attacks because the Establishment doesn't understand conservative arguments.

Inner city Republican candidates are often afraid to talk about guns. Or, worse, they reject conservative positions and join along with the Democrats in voicing anti-gun rhetoric. They figure since so many people are dying from gun violence in their districts, the voters *must* be anti-gun. It's a wrongheaded assumption.

Even among blue collar voters – in many ways, *especially* among blue collar voters – private gun ownership is a very sensitive issue. This voting bloc may vote Democrat, but they include many hunters. Many blue collar citizens also live in crime-ridden inner cities, where gun ownership is a way of protecting ones' home when the police can't be everywhere. They understand the fact that a right to self defense is part of the American ethos!

Why aren't Republicans taking advantage of this?

You may have heard about Colorado's recent recall elections. Three Democrat state senators were turned out of office in Democrat-heavy districts on a wave of public dissatisfaction. The Republicans gained two senators in Democrat districts. Each election was the result of both, legislators losing touch with their constituency and overreaching anti-gun measures.

Senate District 3, in Pueblo, was perhaps the most groundbreaking. Almost half the voters in the district are Democrats, with Republicans and Independents splitting the other half. The district is overwhelmingly lower income and Hispanic. Yet a Republican was able to turn a Democrat out of office, largely because of bad votes on guns.

Democrats "own" the pro-illegal immigrant debate. They think it's a net advantage because they expect those immigrants will become Democrat voters once they naturalize. But most Americans are opposed to an unsecure border and mass surges of people entering the country illegally. In an age of terrorism it takes on even a more urgent cast.

But instead of capitalizing on this, Establishment Republicans in Washington are trying to "defuse" the negatives of the issue by doing their own versions of amnesty. Yes, it is a delicate issue because of the potential to be misunderstood as racist. But who, *exactly*, thinks border security is racist? *White liberals!* White liberals who aren't going to vote Republican if you paid them. Hispanic American citizens, by and large, support a legal process to acquire citizenship, not amnesty.

As will be explained later in this chapter, even opposition to minimum wage increases can work in favor of Republicans, too, if messaged properly.

Even on "growth" issues – limiting housing and business construction – Republicans can win. When Democrats in Colorado pressed their new majority in the Senate to push for strict limits on who could build what, where, Republican legislators stood up to them. The Democrat proposals were so outrageous that 12 of 13 daily newspapers in Colorado sided with Republicans against the plan. Even the media can be won over, with the right approach.

But the most interesting thing about that experience, which I was part of (on legislative media staff at the time), was that Hispanic Democrat legislators also voted with Republicans. Why?

As much as progressive liberals try to deny that capitalism works, housing costs are subject to market conditions. If there aren't enough houses to meet demand, then the value of existing housing goes up – it's more rare. If no one can build new houses, it puts a hard ceiling on the number of housing units and the cost of homes will skyrocket. Apartments too. Property taxes, too. All this hurts the elderly, people on fixed incomes, and people who've lived in their houses for a long period of time hardest. Many of Colorado's Hispanics would have been hit by at least one of those cost increases.

Hispanic legislators also voted often with Republicans on school choice issues – their students were too disadvantaged to be trapped in failing schools without the option to take classes elsewhere.

Republicans should take the initiative on environmental issues by emphasizing the "conservation" aspect of conservatism. Too much of the Republican anti-environmental reputation has been driven by corporatism anyway, not by true conservative pro-business ideals. A true conservative safeguards limited or renewable resources so as not to exhaust them.

A bitter anti-fracking (drilling for oil/gas by fracturing the rock strata) initiative in Colorado went nowhere because of all the jobs that would be at stake if it were curtailed. Environmental issues don't all favor Democrats. We should stop acting like they do.

Don't give up on any audience or district. Sometimes districts and states where Democrats are always in charge are the best places to spread conservative ideas because no one is more familiar with the pitfalls of Democrat policies – the lost jobs, the rising crime rates, the failing schools, the crushing tax burdens – than people who live in the Democrat "ghettos." That's a huge potential expansion market for the right candidate with the right message.

Republicans have at our disposal a huge repertoire of issues we can talk about. Let's talk about them!

Experts a decade ago predicted a move of voters away from principled positions. Establishment Republicans were certainly moving away from them, to take advantage of the perceived shift.

But then came the Tea Party revolution – a movement of people basically saying, "Do what you promised, don't govern by the other side's rules. Use conservative principles!" It transformed politics.

Ignore "conventional wisdom" that says candidates in competitive districts need to move as far toward the center as possible. We are far better off if candidates of strong principle are running, because they energize the base and gain the respect of independents and moderates who appreciate people of strong conviction.

Principle is not dead. It is valuable.

Moderates are killing the GOP by stifling its powerful message.

Don't Be That Guy

A course on "what not to do" for politicians can be told as a story of three US Senate candidates from Colorado.

One year, Colorado had a big-ticket candidate who had served for a decade as one of the few "life at conception" ideologues in Congress. Everyone knew he was one of the most steadfast members of Congress on abortion and every other conservative issue. He had a reputation.

But when he ran for the US Senate and was asked to support Personhood for unborn children, he first balked, then publicly came out against it. His campaign manager was intentionally running him as a "centrist!"

Seriously?

It was inexplicable. He didn't want to be labeled an "extremist" by endorsing something he had outwardly supported his whole career!

More than half the state's Republican activists that year (the delegates who voted at assemblies to draft the GOP platform) supported Personhood. It was disastrous to his candidacy for him to come out against it.

It made people question who he really was, and what he believed.

That candidate made the mistake of "running from his record," which effectively meant he was also running away from his base! He had been told, incorrectly, that he needed to moderate his stance if he was to have any chance of being elected.

It didn't do him any good. Unfortunately for him, the Democrats *remembered* his former record (shock!), and used it in campaign ads. Meanwhile, the candidate's own base started to believe he had really changed his positions (which he might have), and *they* abandoned him to a significant enough degree that it cut into his support.

He underperformed the GOP presidential candidate by 80,000 votes (3.5% of the vote)!

So he got a triple whammy – he lost conservatives because he abandoned his record, and he lost moderates for two reasons. One, he'd once held the positions mentioned in the Democrat attack ads, which wouldn't be as damaging except... Two, he'd calculatingly "moderated" his position, which in the minds of independent and critically minded voters meant he *was admitting* he should never have believed those things! *Therefore those issues instantly became indefensible!*

Finally, by moderating his stance, so as not to appear extreme, *he essentially labeled his strongest supporters as extreme!* Nice way to backhand your friends and allies!

They didn't appreciate that.

Another US Senate candidate learned from the mistakes of the first. He took a position which was essentially supportive of Personhood, and he was able to win a primary against an opponent who was nationally recognized as "pro-life" but who held to rape/incest exceptions. Colorado pro-lifers rejected her and voted for him.

Now, this US Senate candidate developed a loyal following early on because he was a straight shooter. He said boldly what he believed and he didn't back down. He could usually explain his positions so people respected any differences they might hold. He was Reaganesque.

Then he started getting pressure from the media, and from non-stop Democrat ads, and his poll numbers started dropping.

He blinked!

He reversed himself on Personhood and started floundering, trying to take a new position that wasn't what he really believed, but was what he thought the people wanted to hear. He started backing away from other positions, as they got attacked in the press and on the airwaves.

Not only did he get "the triple whammy" the earlier candidate got – 1) he's not winning votes because he once *had* held that "extreme" position, 2) he is losing his base because they wonder where he stands, 3) he's labeled his supporters extreme, and any other candidate who stuck by the "extreme" positions.

And he also gave up the advantage of personal gravitas. He was no longer the "straight shooter" who spoke boldly and with confidence. He was off balance and looked wishy-washy. It was a completely different image from the one that had sustained him through the primary.

He also lost.

In 2014 we have yet another US Senate candidate. In the Colorado legislature he had made a name for himself as a favorite of all the conservative groups – social conservatives, fiscal conservatives, etc. He was solid. He was the guy you knew you could count on.

When he was elected to Congress, he got "Washingtonitis." He caught the Establishment disease so many conservative Republicans seem to get once they have an office away from their home state.

Then soon after he became the Republican candidate for US Senate he announced he was no longer supporting Personhood for the unborn child. What's more, he thought he'd be clever and defuse the "birth control" issue (i.e. the myth that Personhood will ban "contraceptives") by announcing he favored "over-the-counter" birth control! He made no distinction between true contraceptives and abortifacients. All over the counter? Not to mention these are potentially dangerous high dose drugs. Without a doctor's advice?

Again, it was the same old story. He didn't pick up much support from moderates, because they knew he once believed those things. He's getting constant ads calling him "extreme" on abortion, no matter what his new position is. His support from the base – formerly his strongest allies – has gone all wiggly. They're trained, so most will vote for him, but how many won't? And he's essentially calling his former supporters and every other Colorado candidate who still supports Personhood "extreme."

Ironically, even though he's become the most abortion-neutral nominee for US Senate in the state's recent memory, he's getting *more* attack ads against him as an extremist because *his flip-flopping has simply drawn attention to his former positions!*

Don't be that guy who backs away from solid conservative stands on issues. It'll only hurt you.

Don't avoid staking out solid, uncompromised principles – embrace them!

The best way to react when your principled positions are attacked as "extreme" is to simply explain why the positions are not extreme, but rather are common sense.

That was Reagan's strength.

Don't run away – educate!

Voters will often respect your views, even if they disagree with you, so long as they know your views are sincerely held and your other positions are generally on mark with what they're looking for.

This is why Ronald Reagan did so well.

The Truth Doesn't Matter to Democrats

I'm astonished to see not all candidates understand this – and obviously not all campaign managers.

They will be tagged with the extremist label whether they qualify or not.

Every year, never fail, Democrats will accuse Republicans of hating women, wanting poor people to starve, being racists, wanting rich people to pay no taxes and wanting to turn rivers into cesspools.

They will run ads to accuse candidates of all these things, regardless of how conservative or moderate they are in real life.

Republicans have a hard time believing this, because we are so focused on facts, and truth.

"Well, that's not technically correct. In actuality..."

Nevertheless, we see supposedly principled politicians rushing to moderate their public positions – racing to the center – every election cycle. They naively think they can avoid the "extremist" label if they keep their statements and public issue positions moderate enough. It's tragicomic when candidates who've *established* themselves as conservatives in the past try to rebrand themselves as "centrists."

It doesn't fool the voters, unless they want to be fooled. It only proves to them you're playing a game with them, and you don't stand by fixed principles. It adds to the cynicism in politics today. Such hypocrisy makes people – young people especially – leery of ever voting for a Republican.

Democrats also know that if they muddy the waters enough, sincere independents won't know *what* the truth is.

In Ben Shapiro's book, *How to Debate Leftists and Destroy Them*, he says the GOP is the ideas party, and the Democrats aren't. In a straight out contest of ideas, the Democrats can't compete. That's why they lie. Shapiro says if you can inoculate yourself from the attacks, and defuse their lies and distortions, they will have nothing else – no facts – to fall back upon.

The Blueprint is a book by Adam Schrager and Rob Witwer that has gained national notoriety as an analysis of the way Democrats leveraged coordinated campaigns, funded by millions of dollars funneled through political issue groups, to essentially buy key legislative races and take over control of chambers in the Colorado state legislature.

The campaign in 2000 which flipped control of the State Senate (I was involved in one of the losing Republican campaigns, and got to watch the disaster develop from the inside) benefited from four multi-millionaires with progressive ideals and the determination to use their money in the election to further their agenda. Over the course of 30 months, *The Blueprint* says, they "invested" $110 million in several key races – *an unheard of amount of money* at that time in Colorado politics.

It changed the lay of the land at the Capitol. But perhaps the main outcome, which I'm sure was intended, is that it gave Democrats control over the Congressional and legislative redistricting process in the state, for the first time ever.

The book has been used by many Establishment Republicans as support for their "jobs and economy" focus – as a lesson to steer away from "divisive social issues." In fact, the Democrat takeover had a lot more to do with outspending Republicans, targeting issue-based voter blocs and mutual coordination than it did with message.

What lessons *can* be taken about messaging in those campaigns is more to show how untruthful Democrat ads were – intentionally so.

Also in *The Blueprint*, former Colorado House Majority Leader Keith King points to two legislative candidates whose positions were very different on support for traditional public school models vs. school choice. "The Democratic 527s were running exactly the same kind of ads against both of them. So that tells me that the Democratic campaign had nothing to do with issues, but was about winning at all costs. Regardless of the values of our candidates, the Democrats would smear them."

The Blueprint goes on, having spoken to the Democrat legislators in charge of the "Roundtable" campaign to take over the state legislature. "Although internally, Roundtable members described [Rep. Ramey] Johnson as 'a moderate,' their eventual strategy would focus on painting her as an extreme conservative."

Why do they persist in lying?

Because they know it works to galvanize their base.

In the summer of 2014, during the IRS vs. Tea Party corruption hearings in Congress, why did the Obama Administration make the unlikely claim that dozens of IRS hard drives had crashed and deleted all their (incriminating) e-mails? Why make such an obvious, bald-faced assertion of falsehood?

Because they knew they could get away with it!

They know millions of Americans will be outraged at such deception – their "above the law" contempt. But *those* millions of Americans were *already* outraged long before the IRS exposure.

Democrats know millions of people who are inclined to support their socialist president, Barack Obama, won't believe *any* criticism of him, no matter how well founded and evidenced.

Democrat lies lose them nothing, and they gain a great deal.

Contrast – Using Ideas and Emotion

Who's heard that political ad on TV where one candidate says, "My opponent is kind of a moderate, and he's not bad on some of the issues, but I'm a little different from him on these three things..."

Haven't heard it? Why do you suppose that is?

Politics is a game of contrasts, far more than comparisons. Certainly not a game of degrees – not in the public-influencing rhetoric, anyway.

If your opponent takes a stand and you don't then explain how you differ from his or her opinion, the voter has no reason to think voting for you would be any different than voting for him or her.

In a battle of ideas, contrast is critical. Why *should* a voter choose one over the other? The less contrast you present, between one candidate and another, or between one party and the other, the more reason a voter has to see "R" or "D" as the *only* contrasting factor.

And many cynical voters figure there's not much contrast there, either!

This is why the Establishment fails to motivate voters. They have lessened the contrast between Republicans and Democrats, and between Republican and Democrat ideas.

It's also why conservatives, properly educated and prepared, are likely to do much better in a contest of contrasts. *Real* differences between ideas.

If you're in a room of political activists it's certainly possible to provide contrast by simple explanation – "they believe 'A,' whereas I believe 'B,' and this is why..."

But most voters in this day and age of sound bites and constant distraction aren't going to be able to pay attention to a long, turgid explanation of why your way's better.

It's easier if you can put it into writing. Then, at least, many voters will examine the literature and try to compare and contrast that way. The problem here is how many lies are liable to be in your opponents' literature – charges you can't address in print because it's not a responsive media.

Much of voter behavior is emotional. Democrats use this every election.

"I care about you more than the other guy does."

Psychologists will tell you that people remember emotional things. If you can get your ideas to a voter through an emotional argument or a personal connection, they're more likely to remember your ideas and how they contrast with the other side's ideas.

Ronald Reagan understood better than most Republicans of his day and ours that he had to touch the American people on an emotional level. He didn't talk in scientific or theoretical terms about how a particular policy would be better than another.

Sure, he *did*, but not exclusively.

And he typically used a humorous or poignant story when he did. Something people would remember.

Reagan's gift was being able to recognize how those intellectual policies affected individual Americans, for better or worse, and he knew how to sincerely express empathy with those individuals so *they* knew he understood how government impacts *them*.

I mentioned in an earlier chapter that moderate Republicans have a hard time connecting not just with the conservative base, but also with newly activated voters, like many members of the Tea Party who weren't even interested in politics before President Obama started screwing with their lives.

Many Tea Party voters got activated in politics *for the first time* after Obama became president. Why? Because they lost their jobs, or their small businesses suffered setbacks due to the economic downturn, government intrusion, or the flicker-fast, unpredictable changes to government regulations that negatively affected them.

A moderate, Establishment Republican will have a hard time connecting with these newly energized and activated citizens because they don't personally understand the *highly* principled conservative realizations that drew these Tea Party voters into politics in the first place.

Many new activists are *very* emotional about what happened. A job loss is personal. A small business is very personal.

And most of them understand pretty well what happened – how a poorly run government affected them – and how to fix it.

These voters are emotionally and financially invested in how government intrudes into their lives, and the Establishment candidates – who often believe it's a good thing for government to involve itself by funding and regulating business – don't grasp the concepts that motivate these voters.

But it sure matters to those voters whether you hold a right or wrong opinion on how to fix things.

But Republicans put themselves at a potential disadvantage when they train candidates to focus only on fiscal issues.

Jobs and the economy can only carry a candidate so far if the economy is doing well. "I'll keep things going the way they are," is a much less compelling statement than, "Things are going to hell in a handbasket with the Democrats' policies – I'm going to change that!"

And running on fiscal issues doesn't work very well if the economy is doing badly and Republicans are in charge. In 2008, the "jobs and economy" issue worked better for Obama than for Republicans, because so many people blamed Bush and the war for the state of things.

We have to broaden our toolkit. Don't get locked into one formula.

Family issues like marriage and abortion work for the Republican Party because they *are* emotional issues. A politician mentioning these issues touches a family voter's heart because those citizens have a visceral investment.

Family voters see the breakdown of the family due to a loss of morals, a corrosive mass media, a disappearing sense of personal responsibility, an increased dependence upon government and a reduced respect for the value of human life.

They see government policy impact their lives and their family in terms of what their children are taught, how their children behave and the ways their children think. Not just that, but they see *financial impacts* as the breakdown of the traditional family unit create single-parent homes and poverty which then falls back on them as taxpayers to pay for.

Family voters see their family paying for the breakdown of society, personally and financially.

That's very emotional. Connecting with these voters empathetically works in a way that an egghead Establishment bean counter can't even conceive.

Much of communicating with voters is finding issues which relate to taking care of a person's family and what kind of a world they're going to leave their children. This is also why I don't believe even today's feeding frenzy of government assistance and dependence is a permanent condition. Someday those people are going to realize the consequences.

Today's Tea Party is the strongest force within the GOP constellation that's actually taking a stand on the issues that make up the Republican Party platform. Though they concentrate primarily on economic issues, some elements within the Tea Party do a better job than others incorporating social conservative issues into the argument.

And "allied" groups, such as the 9/12 Committees fully embrace the entire GOP platform, including points of social conservatism.

For these reasons it's candidates from this wing of the party that *should* be more successful than Establishment candidates in November. They can talk in a way that connects.

Unless we can set up a clear contrast between our views and the views of our opponents, Republicans can't catch the attention of the public, and can't engage the hearts and minds of people who will turn out to vote.

Perhaps more importantly, without that contrast we cannot build our movement, because we convince no one – no young people, especially – that our side is better.

We have to talk about why we believe what we do. Or at least just bring up the controversy so inquiring minds want to understand how the sides differ.

"Perceived" contrast" isn't sufficient, because hypocrisy will soon turn people away. Actual, sincere differences on major policy issues must be defined in order to cultivate a new generation of conservatives.

Columnist and speaker Michelle Malkin has made the point that if we remain silent on major issues, we allow Democrats to define us however they like. We leave the field open to them. That's the main reason Republican candidates have experienced a ridiculous degree of difficulty getting the public to catch fire on their candidacies.

It's one of the most central points of electoral politics – if you can't set up a real contrast between you and your opponent, why would anyone vote for you? Candidate schools continuously harp on having a ready answer when asked why you're running. This should be a *softball* for Republican candidates!

We're the ideas party! Not the Democrats. No way!

Republicans have real, common sense ideas – ideas that actually work, and aren't exclusively based in spending money or playing off irrational emotion.

And Americans appreciate when someone has the confidence and courage to express their views openly, even when those positions might differ from what the audience expects to hear. People respect that.

Remember in an earlier chapter about compromise, I mentioned how candidates train their supporters, because those people who have invested in their candidacy feel a need to defend their positions? This can be turned to our advantage, too.

If a strong conservative candidate is running for president, or senate, or any office to a lesser degree, he or she has the power to train their supporters in how to be a conservative.

This extends, to a lesser degree, to engaged voters. There are other voices training voters, and we have to compete with that. But our ideas are stronger, and with proper messaging we can prevail.

A Republican should be able to say he or she is running because we have the solutions for America's problems, and here they are!

That can be transformational, because it leads people to see your ideas as vehicles of change. Contrast that against the opponents' status quo, and you're on your way.

Inspiration

The Establishment's strategy for gaining more votes is to have their candidates change their message to match what the average targeted voter wants to hear.

Instead – as example after example has shown, from Ronald Reagan to Winston Churchill to Franklin Roosevelt, etc. – candidates and leading officials should be aiming to change peoples' minds to match their *own* visionary ideas, policies and principles!

That's what leadership is, though few in government today realize that.

You cannot win if you have no vision for victory. If you're sure you're going to lose, you will convey that impression to those who are watching.

You'll lose! Self fulfilling prophecy.

That's largely why President Jimmy Carter was such a dismal president, and why voters turned him out of office. He presented an image of himself as just another citizen at the mercy of events and situations beyond his control, and he transmitted his own depression and demoralization to the public at large.

Stagflation! Terrorism! Gas prices! The sky is falling! Re-elect me!

Why?

Thinking back to the "Don't Be That Guy" subchapter, remember what I said about running away from your positions? When a candidate does that – distances herself from policy positions or ideas that she once espoused – *it's like telegraphing to the voting public that she doesn't believe her own rhetoric, and she believes those positions and ideas are losers!*

"Well, *dolt*, then why were you urging me, two years ago, to *believe* you?!"

When President Franklin Roosevelt announced the Pearl Harbor attack, and that the United States was at war, he dwelt on the damage and the infamy. He wasn't trying to depress Americans. He was giving them reason to be angry.

Then he channeled that outrage into support for a long war. At that moment, it was entirely unclear to many whether the United States could win or not. He was setting up the challenge, which wasn't a small one. But he also presented a determination and a confidence that we would overcome.

In fact, through the first six months of America's involvement in World War II, the news was mainly hearing of fresh defeats at the hands of Japan, not to mention dire reports from the battlefields of Europe, too.

But FDR never flagged in providing material to inspire his people to resist, to build, to hope that we would come back and ultimately see victory against our enemies.

He used the language of inspiration during the Great Depression, too. "The only thing we have to fear is fear itself!"

In announcing his New Frontier program, President John F. Kennedy hearkened back to the former frontier – the historic adventure of making of America – and invited Americans to join in the exciting opportunity of building their own future today. Participating in their own adventure, which would be remembered by their children and beyond.

Martin Luther King Jr.'s "I Have a Dream" speech followed the inspirational formula. Set up the challenge, lay out a plan, and encourage listeners to believe that it's possible to achieve – tell them that they will accomplish the goal. The key was that *he had a dream*, and motivated people to share not just in the vision, but in the effort to reach that ideal.

One of the most important parts of inspiration is convincing people they have the power to change their world. In a speech in 1967, having just been elected Governor of California, he said, "We are being watched; watched by those all across this land who once again dare to believe that our concept of responsible people-oriented government can work as the Founding Fathers meant it to work. If we can prove that here, we can start a prairie fire that can sweep across this country."

He sets up the challenge – a "conventional wisdom" that such things are *not* possible, that that's a dream whose time is past – then provides hope and a path to victory. It's inspiration at its grandest.

I find it astonishing, in one respect, that he had such vision more than a decade before that prairie fire reached Washington DC. But in another sense, in retrospect, we know that he had such a vision, because he instilled it in all of us who remember him fondly.

Reagan had an unfailing optimism, and compelled people to see his vision through the force of his personality. "America's best days are yet to come. Our proudest moments are yet to be. Our most glorious achievements are just ahead."

There is a balance to be had. The goals we set must be realistic. People must be able to believe.

But the ideas also cannot be mundane or too small. No one is inspired by the status quo.

The best speeches – the best visions – require a suspension of disbelief. They must not be so fantastic people dismiss them out of hand. An inspirational speech or platform must see what others cannot see or hope for without urging. It lifts them beyond normal perception.

But a realistic person must be able to see the accomplishment of that dream in their mind. That's what makes them believe, and what inspires them to follow.

Newt Gingrich, as House Minority Leader, used inspiration when he crafted the Contract With America – it presented a challenge, set up a realistic plan to overcome, and included the vision to make it happen. It was a brilliant way to capitalize on ideas and inspiration to win an election.

And it worked!

The key here is this. A useful vision often strains the bounds of grounded reality – it is, literally, *visionary*. But when leaders are able to use inspirational language, they can lead people to accomplish unrealistic, seemingly impossible things.

History is replete with examples of this, from America's winning independence from the world's largest empire to man walking on the Moon.

How do you inspire someone? Tell them what's possible – even if it's *not*, strictly – set up a realistic plan to accomplish it, and give them a vision so they can believe success is possible.

Combine ideas and inspiration and the ideas *become* the inspiration. But only if they're fresh, realistic, and presented in a visionary way.

It is the job of any conservative candidate to inspire society through the education they provide through speeches, ads, etc., and to reinforce these challenging ideas with the emotional connections they make.

Messaging

Democrats have it easy. Their ideas are, by their nature, very simple and easy to explain. Even if they don't work. Many of their ideas start off at an emotional level.

Often, that's all they are! No logic, just emotion, like a child.

If the problem is that it's too cold, their solution is to turn up the heat. Being cold is an emotional issue for anyone who's cold. So Democrats cry out, "Turn up the heat!" and never have to distract voters with explanations of how to pay for the increased cost of electricity or heating gas.

If the problem is that we're at war, Democrats' answer seems to be to end the war. *Really?* Go tell our enemies to end the war. See how that works out. But ending the war – absent any consideration of worldly realities – is the simplest and most emotionally appealing argument.

Their solutions are popular because most voters aren't even going to consider the deeper implications of the policy solutions offered. They figure the simple solution is exactly what needs to happen, so why not do it?

Republicans often get stuck explaining, intellectually, why the Democrats' simple ideas have obscure, but very important, unintended consequences. Explaining these things is hard. Republicans try to do it anyway, because they don't know what else to do.

"Turn up the heat" is a better sound bite for an ad than, "It costs too much," because you'd have to explain *how* it costs too much.

The trick is to boil down the essence of why the Democrat plan won't work or the Republican plan will. Find a memorable sound bite and hit it. A one-liner, like you'd see in a great televised debate, or a classic Humphrey Bogart movie.

Hmm… Movies.

Reagan had an unfair advantage. He was an actor, and he realized politics requires showmanship.

He had another advantage. He had run a union (the Screen Actors Guild). Tough labor negotiations require analysis of the problem and the levers that might change minds or trigger concessions. Once those targets are identified, press those buttons hard and you've got it.

I have a confession to make. I was raised a Republican during the Reagan years. But when I was in high school and college I had flirtations with progressive ideology. I always called myself a moderate. But the call of the simple logic of Democrat policy ideas – aid the poor, fight racism, make rich people pay their fair share, assign government agencies to every problem – caused me to turn to the Democrats because I believed (as my teachers and the news media suggested) Republicans were the party of the rich and uncaring.

One year my aunt and uncle gave me Sen. Barry Goldwater's (R-AZ) autobiography as a Christmas gift. It's not something I would have chosen to read, but I was a political junkie and I thought it'd be interesting.

Before I read that book I'd never realized that Democrats and Republicans often – not always – identify the same problems in society that need to be solved. They just have *very different* proposed solutions.

Nevertheless, once presented in a coherent manner, I was impressed at how logical the Republican solutions were, and how easily many of those Democrat solution proposals were refuted. It was a paradigm shift for me – I suddenly realized why Republicans believed and acted as they did. I'd always assigned ulterior motives, but once I understood the philosophy everything began to make sense. It wasn't an immediate process – it took years.

With our audience it still might take years, not months or weeks. But we reap what we sow. The Establishment has been asleep at the wheel for years. We have catchup sowing to do! It will pay off later, if not now.

Later, I was promoted into middle management, and realized from the inside looking out that a lot of affluent people got that way through hard work, and express appreciation for their wealth through charity and goodwill toward their employees. At the same time I realized that, while many "working class" people are also hard workers, aiming to make a better life for themselves and their families, others were more interested in shirking work and taking advantage of their employers than they were in doing a good job.

Again, it provoked a paradigm shift which brought me back toward conservative principles. The more I learned, the stronger I became in my beliefs. Gingrich's Contract With America solidified by return to the Republican Party.

In the fullness of maturity I've realized the Democrats aren't always wrong, and Republicans aren't always right. Not even conservatives. But conservative ideas certainly are right ten times more often than they're wrong.

That's where Republicans have the edge, via their conservative party platform. It's possible to reach people – young people especially – through education and outreach, and bring them over to our side.

All those years the reason I "wandered" politically and didn't identify as a Republican was because Republicans had failed miserably at messaging their ideas to me. Or their messaging didn't penetrate. It's certainly possible they tried and weren't able to get through my "filters," which included the news media and my teachers' expressed political opinions and biases.

I do really think they weren't trying, though, or they weren't trying the right message. I was pretty politically aware, and if I'd heard the right arguments I would have responded.

Republicans are bad at overthinking, overanalyzing, overexplaining. I'm guilty of this myself.

The American public suffers from "MEGO" disease – My Eyes Gloss Over. If you can't communicate with them effectively in a short and relatively simple way, most people just won't pay attention.

So in order to effectively communicate with that worker-voter a Republican has to keep it simple and keep it focused.

Simple ad: Voter: "You want $15/hr? Why not? I'm not paying the bills." GOP: "Actually, you *are!*"

Minimum wage increases are bad for workers, and it's because 1) you might lose your job because you're more expensive, and 2) the cost of goods is going to go up because they cost more to produce, and consumers will shop less, which means no pay increase for the worker, and less job security.

The cost of doing business argument works with consumer voters, too.

Most ads and speeches from the GOP Establishment fail to excite voters. Why?

Partly it's because they don't quickly connect with the voter, or they only mouth generalizations. Who's against keeping Americans safe?

You've got to talk to voters about what they care about. Or at least make a good case why they *should* care about something, even if they may not already.

Partly it's because there's nothing new in what they say. Who isn't for "improving the economy" or "creating more jobs?" Usually both sides are using those same sound bites. To an average citizen, watching the Democrat and Republican talk in generalities about what they're going to do is like watching the back-and-forth of a tennis match without understanding the rules. It looks like just "he said, she said."

If you're not a policy wonk it's hard to understand how the economy improves using different methods, much less being able to compare one method against another.

It's possible to explain it, yes, but it's not easy and you have to maintain the voter's attention long enough to do it.

Reagan reached people viscerally.

He drew them in emotionally by connecting at a personal level.

The fact is, you're *going* to connect at a personal level, no matter what. You're either going to look like who *you* want to look like, or who *your opponent* wants you to look like. That impression – first, or otherwise – is going to stick with those voters.

You want to look like you're in control, and like you know what you're talking about. As a proponent of conservative ideas, remember these are the ideas that are going to restore America to greatness!

Act like it! Don't apologize for your beliefs.

Rather than trying to find common ground with your opponent, backing away from a charge they've made about how heartless you are for opposing "consumer protections," explain how "anti-business regulations" increase consumer costs and cause higher unemployment!

You have good reasons to believe what you do, and you can explain them, confidently, and in a way that makes sense. To do that, you have to prepare, but if you really believe these things, you've already done that groundwork.

Admirers of Reagan have often heard him called a "hedgehog" – a reference to an essay by Isaiah Berlin which related a Greek saying. "The fox knows many things, but the hedgehog knows one big thing." In other words, he wasn't a complicated thinker, but he knew "one big thing." That one big thing was his grounding conservative philosophy. I would also add his deep faith in God.

Those who worked with Reagan tell us that whenever he was faced with a dilemma he checked his underlying conservative groundings, or his faith, or both, and inherently understood how he should approach something.

He could extrapolate an answer to any question from the "big things" he knew in his heart.

Conservatives should, in any circumstance, be able to refer to these conservative groundings – our foundational philosophies – and come up with an answer. Then you can explain your answer in light of the philosophy to anyone who asks.

Lastly, don't run from a fight – it makes you look weak, like you either don't know what you're talking about, or it makes you look guilty of whatever charge has been made.

Keep the initiative. Stay on offense.

Our candidates are usually impeccably polite, and it works against us. *Sometimes, when faced with an outrageous charge, or policy position, a Republican should be outraged!* And we should be able to explain why we're outraged, and why voters should be too.

General George S. Patton followed a practice Napoleon Bonaparte swore by. As they moved with their armies they would observe the landscape and consider how they had best react if the enemy charged over each hill or ridge at that very moment.

Be ready for it. Don't get caught off guard. Chess – know what moves your opponent is likely to make next.

Patton also believed in a great offense as the best defense. He knew if he kept the initiative and moved faster than his opponents could anticipate he would keep them off balance and they'd never be able to prepare against his assaults.

Make sure your opponent is reacting to your charges, and not the other way around. Be relentless. The Democrats are like that, but in recent years they've become predictable and more easily defended against. It's our turn.

Republican candidates should be challenging their opponents for supporting abortion as birth control, on demand, through 9 months of pregnancy!

Outside of the South, almost every single Democrat candidate holds that position.

Don't allow them to use the specious "birth control" line on you, or the "war on women." *Call them on late term*

181

abortion in a debate! See if they're willing to offend Planned Parenthood by saying differently!

There are many other outrageous policy positions the Democrats hold. We should point those out, and not be polite about it.

Let's be outraged, and let the American people join in!

Conclusion

The Democrats' formula for winning elections is simple, like their party platform. Demonize Republicans, truthfully or not. Make it look like they're greedy, corrupt puppets who are tone-deaf to the average working person in America. Mobilize unions to do your footwork for you. Call upon rich "limousine liberals" who will send huge checks, or fund enormous independent expenditures while not holding it against your party that it demagogues the status of being wealthy. Rely upon the news media to cover up your every fault, and to advertise your every initiative as pure common sense and inspirational leadership. Spend lots of money. Lots. And when you run out, raise taxes "on the rich" again and again until you have enough money to spend more and more on these problems that never seem to get solved doing it "your way."

For Republicans it's more complicated. There's no set formula. It's a matter of connecting with the hearts of the American people. But it's more than that. You have to reach the American peoples' hearts through their brain, which complicates the procedure.

But we have the advantage in most of the aspects of winning elections. We should never assume the Democrats hold all the cards.

The Democrats, today, use lies, emotion and giveaways (government programs) to attract new voters and keep the ones they have. These are each very powerful tools, and should never be underestimated.

We, on the other hand, have the most recent inspiring leader – Ronald Reagan – who Americans can generally agree upon and revere. Many Democrats feel very inspired by Obama, but he has such strong negatives among a huge percentage of the population that he cannot qualify as an inspiring American leader. Again, many Democrats hold Bill Clinton in high esteem, but Obama has largely displaced Bill. His positives among Democrats and his negatives among Republicans have subsided over time, replaced by strong feelings on both sides for or against Obama.

Democrats really have to go back to either John F. Kennedy or Harry Truman to find a standard bearer who was generally liked and fondly remembered by a large segment of the US population.

Conservatives definitely have real ideas and workable solutions on their side. The GOP is the ideas party not because of any ideas but conservative ideas provided by Goldwater and Reagan.

Conservatives can draw upon voter attachment to emotional matters such as pocketbook (jobs, economy, prosperity) and family issues to help us.

And, perhaps more importantly, when it comes right down to it, Americans are a rational, level headed, common sense people. And when emotion is removed from the argument – hard to do, but it often happens – a majority of Americans will understand that Republican and conservative proposals are more rational and common sense than Democrat progressive proposals.

Both parties have the potential for successful messaging and inspiration. The Democrats have recently been more successful at both, but there's nothing to say that couldn't change with a little tweaking and training.

Let's work on that!

It's crucial that we fix what's wrong on our side and put a new plan of communication into action.

The Establishment has shown they are inept. They are the problem.

The Tea Party can rise above and lead both the GOP and the United States into a new generation of prosperity and *real* progress.

Chapter 10
How to Train Your Politician

Self government is at the core of our Constitutional system and at the foundation of the government our Framers set up for us.

The very words of that Constitution were written to limit our *government*, not the people. That government is best which governs least, and all that.

Self government is at the heart of the concept of representative government. If we do not express ourselves and our ideas, and elect representatives who will carry those expressions to the place of government – be it Washington D.C., our state capitol, or our town hall – we have failed in self government, and we no longer have a functioning representative democracy.

Benjamin Franklin was asked, emerging from weeks of deliberations at the Constitutional Convention, "Have we got a republic, or a monarchy?" He replied, "A republic, if you can keep it."

Do we intend to keep it?

If we do not stand up for ourselves, instead allowing our leaders to run amok, representing others but not us, how are we to self govern?

Our representative democracy is not functioning. And it's our fault!

You Are the Quality Control Division

Our representatives are supposed to be accountable.

But if we won't hold them to account, we are not doing our duty, and we allow them to run amok.

They become accountable to − beholden to − people and interests *who are not us!*

Granted, one might easily interject, our republic was already battered and bloody before we even came of age. Our present day institutions, many of them, have progressed far beyond any intent of the Framers.

But we can stand up for what we still have. The Constitution was designed to be resilient. It is not a fragile document. It can bounce back if we take care to restore it.

My fear is that citizens of our philosophy − of our conservative values − have been so busy treating the Democrats as the enemy and concentrating on winning every election by whatever means possible, in a "Hungry Hungry Hippo" frenzy (young folks, look it up on YouTube − you'll see the analogy), that we've lost sight of the fact that members of our *own* party are doing violence to the Constitution and processes of self government every day.

Introspection is necessary, and *cannot* be put off for another day when it might seem easier to fix things. If we ever reach that "easy" day, the impetus for improvement will be less urgent.

We have to clean our own house. We must prevent it from being used as a platform for the very destruction we fear.

Only if conservatives accept the responsibility and stand up for our values inside and outside of our comfortable party structure can we hope to restore the American Republic.

But this doesn't have to be a coercive process. We can use honey and a carrot as well as a stick.

Many candidates and officials are happy to do as their constituents want. Just ask them to adopt a higher standard than they've been previously held to. Many of them, in my experience, will do so.

If they need more than asking, use the resolution process (the process used for developing a party platform for most or all states) to indicate how widespread support for these platform ideas within the grassroots who elect your candidates. Most candidates and officials will see the demand and respond.

Altogether, these things will bring along most candidates and officials.

But as the idea of intentional voting catches on, and candidates are rejected in primaries or even in general elections because they were insufficiently conservative, future candidates will take note.

The higher the standards candidates are held to, when they first announce, when they compete in the primary, and even when they're struggling to win in November, the more candidates will want to be "that guy who's right on target." Setting a higher bar will attract more solid candidates.

The 2014 Elections

One side effect of following the practice of intentional voting is that not every Republican who might have won will still win. Some may lose. Sometimes even control of a chamber may be lost, or not be gained. This prospect horrifies Establishment Republicans, as well as anyone still under the thrall of their "party first" training.

Let it go. Calm down. Take comfort in the fact that the Republicans who don't win are the squishes – the people who would have voted (partially) for the Democrat policies anyway. It's a necessary part of cleaning house.

In order to prepare the party for victory in 2016, we have to at least give the party a foretaste of intentional voting in 2014. We have to show them that we will retaliate against RINOs and others who betray the base of the party.

The 2014 elections are expected – and by all means *should* be – a "wave election." Anti-Obama sentiment should sweep the country and millions of people who regularly vote Democrat should instead vote Republican because they're so angry and disgusted with the way things have been run.

But already, in October, we're seeing signs that the Republican lead is soft. Predictions are wavering – maybe the Republican will win this race, or maybe the Democrat will barely hold on. They're even talking about whether the GOP will actually take control of the Senate, as was expected.

Maybe the wave will happen or maybe it won't.

If it doesn't, many will blame this book and sentiments such are expressed here. Some will blame me, personally – it's happened before, and will again.

Such claims are silly and petty. The only way this book could affect the election, one way or another, is if it becomes a bestseller in the next 4 weeks. If it *does*, then what does that tell you about the mood of conservatives in America right now?

In 1994, Americans voted for Speaker Newt Gingrich and the Contract With America as much as they did for their local and statewide Republican candidates. They voted for an idea – an improved spirit and attitude, an example of inspiring leadership.

In 2014, if Republicans don't catch "the wave," it's because Speaker John Boehner and Sen. Mitch McConnell were uninspiring and tentative in leadership. Boehner has actually claimed to be "Obama's best friend," and McConnell is acting like he is, too. They've been trying to wrangle Republicans to support Obama's policies and agenda!!!

There's no "promise" in the GOP – nothing to like, other than that we're "not Obama."

A loss in 2014 will be because the Republicans running failed to earn enough votes, by not following the formulae recommended above for inspiration, conservative messaging, contrast, etc.

We conservatives need to show the Establishment and Republican National Committee they need more than platitudes to win over the base. They need to take action on Republican principles to show us why they deserve our votes. And at the very least, they need to pledge that that's what they'll do, not promising the opposite.

In 2014 and over the next couple of years, we're building and preparing – training – the Republican Party that will hopefully nominate a real conservative for President, and will vanquish the failed policies of progressivism and replace them with a vision for the future. Policies that will work, and will lift America up out of her doldrums and into prosperity once more.

In order to have an America we can be proud of, we need to lay the groundwork now.

We do that by supporting conservatives, not progressives or moderates painted up as conservatives.

An Experiment in Leftism

Without specific, uncompromised standards, not only will true conservatives have a hard time transforming politics, but the parties and candidates are left without a reliable guide to our expectations.

If they don't have a reliable guide to follow, the candidates won't support our specific standards, and those voters who should be on our side will instead be drawn off to support unprincipled "candidates of lesser evil."

It's easy to "stand firm" only during the primary. We're good at that – we fight hard, every primary to get people who will truly represent us and our values.

But when our favored representatives have been defeated and replaced by people who don't represent our views, our fight goes out of us. Our *training* kicks in, and we start putting out our time, effort and emotion to support the people who *don't* represent us!

The Party thinks, "All we have to do is outlast the opposition and push our candidate over the 50 percent line in the primary and these conservatives will support the nominee once more, just like we've trained them."

If you doubt that this is true, let me point you to a Washington Post article from Sep. 21 of this year. In talking about Republicans embracing everything from over-the-counter birth control, to marijuana and higher minimum wages, the Post says, "This year's move to the political middle will serve as a *test* for 2016. If these candidates lose, the party's conservative base is likely to blame it on their straying too far from orthodoxy. If they win, it could provide some evidence that the GOP can expand its coalition by reaching to the center" (italics mine).

Let me translate that for you. It's an experiment (a test, like the article says). They've correctly assessed that *if those candidates who are aggressively positioning themselves toward the center win, then in 2016 we will see a lot* more *candidates running as centrists and leaving conservative platform positions in the dust.*

If these candidates lose, then the experiment has failed and Republican candidates will return to their home, embracing the ideas of conservatism.

If that's not enough for you, consider this deeper implication. For every Republican who campaigns on a non-Republican, leftist platform issue, they're telling the public that they're reasonable and... By extension, make no mistake, they are telling the public the rest of us aren't! They're telling people to vote for them, but not to vote for all those other crazy Republicans – the ones who hold to the party platform – because who would really be so unreasonable as to believe those things?

I assure you – the more public these Republican campaigns with leftist platform items are, especially if they used to be conservative and they've changed their minds – *good, conservative Republicans are going to lose their seats because of them!*

So our officials, on average, and the party's bench of leaders become more progressive in two ways – the successful compromisers become more numerous, and the conservatives will die off from lost elections. *Elections they lost because they got stabbed in the back by someone too cowardly to stand by the party platform.* By someone who told the public Reagan's values were too extreme.

If you reject my characterization of the 2014 elections as an experiment in conflict – if you're having trouble believing that any Republicans should oppose other Republicans, or if you're thinking "the GOP always backs conservatives and moderates alike, in the name of unity" – please think back to 2010 when another experiment was being tried.

The experiment was whether conservative Tea Party candidates could win. The Establishment narrative was that "no, they can't – they're too extreme," and that's the story we heard in the media. But in reality those Tea Party candidates lost because the Establishment bad-mouthed them and told Republicans not to support them.

The Establishment, in 2010, recognized it as an experiment as to whether Tea Party candidates could win, and they knew if these candidates won the Establishment would lose its hold on the minds of the Republican Party. Given that it was a contest that could destroy them, the Republican Establishment put all their efforts into sabotaging these Tea Party candidates, not giving them proper financial support and talking about them in public as "extremists who are going to lose."

Who *does* that, *unless they don't want them to win?*

There's a roadmap for conservatives in all this history.

In 2010 the Establishment recognized they had to go to war against the Tea Party, and we've seen this in evidence ever since. We have to realize we're at war, and respond accordingly.

We *cannot* support those candidates who embrace centrist or leftist positions!

To do so will only encourage them, move them further to the left, raise up others who will do the same, and do great, perhaps permanent harm to the conservative movement!

It may be hard to grasp the need. It may be hard to accept, given our training.

But *we have to ensure that these Republican centrists lose*, or their Establishment experiment will succeed and will set a new permanent tone.

Don't Let Them Train Us, Let's Train Them

We have to think long term – consider what needs to happen eventually, regardless of what may happen even in the current election cycle.

Short term thinking is what got us into this mess in the first place. *We've been teaching the Establishment to ignore us.*

Even if, in our hearts and minds, our beliefs and feelings are quite different, we've fallen into the trap of thinking, "I'll do it, if that's what we have to do to win."

We've acceded to moderate, statist leadership, because when *they* win we've been lying to ourselves, saying, "We won!"

We've demonstrated over and over again it's okay if we don't get what we want.

It seems like every time I suggest that we have to vote against the centrists running in the November elections, most people agree with me, then say "we'll do that next time – for now we need to support every Republican so we can take over the Senate."

I bang my head against the wall. This behavior is what's making things worse and worse for conservatives, election after election.

INTENTIONAL VOTING

What we've been doing is not working. Voting for "any old Republican" in November, no matter what they believe, then trying again in the primary two years later, only to get steamrolled by rich Establishment candidates isn't working.

Unlike Democrats and the Establishment, most true conservatives lack guile. We trust our fellow Republicans, even Establishment people.

We are Charlie Brown, expecting Lucy to hold the ball for us so we can kick a field goal and become the heroes. But Lucy doesn't want us to succeed. She's going to pull the ball away so we can't get what we want this time, or next time, or the time after.

We have to change our game plan. We have to quit being "team players" on a team that despises us. Maybe we change the team leadership, or maybe we change teams.

This is why we must cure ourselves of our "party over principle" reflex, and get over the "lesser of two evils" myth.

It's hard to train yourself not to react by human instinct, and instead do something in a way that seems not to make sense, but will really accomplish what you need. That's what this is – we're almost hard-wired to vote for the lesser of two evils because it seems logical and it's also what the Establishment has trained us to do.

But think about driving a car. If you're sliding on ice toward a cliff, instinct tells you to steer away from the cliff. Experts will tell you that worsens the slide. You're supposed to turn into the slide instead, allowing your tire tread to grip and gain traction.

Airplane pilots know a similar trick. One of the worst situations a pilot can get into is a tailspin. The airplane has stalled, stopped flying, and has become a spinning projectile heading toward the ground. Pilots are taught a non-intuitive remedy – turn the wheel into the spin. This allows the control surfaces to catch hold of the air again, you regain control of the aircraft and pull out of the spin.

We have to pull out of our tailspin, using a non-intuitive remedy. We have to let go of what seems the natural solution – voting Republican, even if he doesn't support the platform – and do the opposite.

We *must* use our votes intentionally in order to influence the character of both, policy and candidates.

We need to un-train ourselves, and re-train ourselves to be consistent with our values, standing up for them at all times, even when our adversaries happen to be members of our very own party.

And we have to turn the tables. We have to start training the party to respond to us!

Standards & Accountability

When your elected officials betray you, are you going to let them get away with it?

The Establishment needs to know that not providing conservatives with a principled nominee will result in loss and disaster for the Party and Establishment candidates.

Otherwise they'll keep disregarding us every election. There have to be consequences for their disdain. And we also must provide them with an incentive to work for our votes by providing principled candidates.

Consequences come first in our training process. Incentives come later, once we have their attention. Once our message has been understood.

In a previous chapter I noted how moderate Republican legislators will demand changes to principled conservative legislation in order to *earn* their vote for legislation? By contrast, conservative voters and legislators are always expected to "suck it up" and support the Establishment agenda "for the good of the party."

Conservatives need to learn from the moderates. *They use their vote as a bargaining chip.*

Votes *are* bargaining chips! That's one main point of this book.

It doesn't work so well in a legislative chamber. Making a deal with a moderate there would usually mean a conservative would have to pledge to support moderate legislation. They'd have to compromise on the party platform in order to get the votes of the moderates on another issue so they'd support principle.

Because of that, the solution is to have a functional majority of conservative legislators in the first place, wherever possible, so they're not dependent on moderate votes. Again, you can see that if you allow an Establishment candidate to win those seats, replacing them with conservatives in order to build a conservative majority becomes more difficult.

Intentional voting is the key to achieving what we need. We as voters must use our votes as bargaining chips – in order to ensure the Party provides candidates who will abide by the Party platform.

If we don't get the candidates we want, the Party leadership has to know our votes won't be there. Providing conservative candidates to vote for must be the price of earning our votes. Otherwise, they will lose.

In many cases, this is true anyway. Moderates often cannot generate the kind of excitement needed to win. It takes a true believer – someone who knows not just what to say, but *why they're saying it!*

The moderate, Establishment candidates have shown that they lose because they cannot show contrast, they cannot inspire, they cannot communicate, and they appear as hypocrites because they don't really believe what they say they believe. They don't meet the smell test. They don't meet the confidence test.

They're cold fish. In general, the American people don't want wishy-washy leaders with no vision for America and who don't really know how to get there.

Besides, without real conservative leadership – without something more than just a few shades different from what the Democrats have been serving up – we're *never* going to get our country back.

Only a true conservative is going to be able to do what must be done. Only a true conservative is going to be able to convince the public of their sincerity, and communicate effectively enough about these ideas to convert the skeptical masses to realize how common sense conservative ideas are.

To get candidates who truly represent us, we must stop acting as "team players" – not for a team that *doesn't* represent us. We have our *own* team, and cooperating with the Establishment means playing for *their* team, not our own.

We have to use the power we have to get what we want. This is called pressure politics.

I know I'm going to be accused by Republicans of "just wanting Republicans to lose."

Some of them, yes. But that's not the point.

I also know some Democrats are going to think, "This is great. They're going to hurt their own moderate candidates so our candidates can win!"

If they think that, they haven't grasped the concept of the book.

The point is for Republicans to get their act together so we can win elections and have another generation – like Reagan's generation – when conservatives are in charge and Americans have confidence in the direction the country is going.

Pressure Politics

For too long, conservatives have been bowing to the politics of fear, as wielded by the Establishment. Fear of what might happen if we don't vote for their people.

They're using fear to pressure us. Don't back down – attack!

We need to be the ones taking the initiative and using the tools of politics in our own favor.

By standing up to them you gain respect. They know they will have to take you into account in the future. You've trained them to pay attention.

The Establishment must fear that if they don't respond to us, we will keep them from getting anything they want. Let them noodle over that for a while. Let them ponder over the consequences of an election gone bad.

Worse, let them contemplate how things might be if *their* party were no longer a majority party – if they threw a party and the conservatives no longer came.

We must set up standards for adherence to conservative principles, tell the candidates we expect them to represent these standards, then hold them to their promises – they cannot diverge from those standards in statements on the campaign trail, nor can they be allowed to vote differently once elected.

Conservative factions who are willing to exert pressure on candidates and officials to embrace solid issue positions is what provides politicians the political courage to avoid compromise.

Candidates are most vulnerable to temptation during the general election, when bad poll numbers or unfavorable press might make them feel a need to back away from firm positions they took during the primary.

Inquiring on candidates' positions early, during the primary when they want to establish their bona fides, gets them on record so they can be held accountable later.

We have to close the deal, solidify the lessons of previous elections, and hold together without flinching, to make sure we have a conservative nominee.

Failing that – if, despite everything we've done to put a conservative over the top, we are still handed a nominee who doesn't believe in the party platform, *we have to be willing to walk away.*

Otherwise, we're never going to have political influence to determine future nominees – we'll always be expected to back down and buckle under and support the Establishment nominees, whether for President, Senate, whatever.

Worse, we'll *expect ourselves* to back down. We won't have the confidence to stand up for ourselves, we'll know those by our sides won't have the strength to carry through, and the arguments that "a conservative can't win" will seem ever more convincing.

Just keep your eye on the ball.

If we support a candidate who professes to be a conservative, and they depart from our standard, we have to be willing to criticize them for it, and call a spade a spade, no matter how it might make that candidate vulnerable in the next election, and no matter whether it might cause them to lose to a candidate from another party.

In fact, we need to keep tabs on things so that we know immediately when they betray us with bad votes or *surprise* changes in their "deeply held political beliefs."

Don't "fly off the handle." Many reports – especially media accounts – are inaccurate. Many times what someone says can be misunderstood. Allow candidates and officials to explain themselves.

But don't let them get away with a different narrative in your presence from what they tell others. Trust, but verify.

If they really have gone "squish," you need to write or call and make sure they know that's not okay.

Politicians don't like to be held accountable. They don't like pressure – it makes them squirm. They may have adverse reactions – they may decide *not* to work with you out of spite.

They have to be made to understand there's a price to be paid for turning their back on you.

When voting for the major party candidate is not an option, we must turn to third party voting in order to make our voice heard. This makes our votes quantifiable – it demonstrates how strong the outrage and outcry is. This also makes our votes identifiable qualitatively – a major party can look at the numbers achieved by a particular third party and understand how they and their candidates would have to change in order to regain those voters.

Reward principle. Punish betrayal. Don't vote for Squishy.

We have to be willing to walk away and denounce that candidate as a lesson to any who will come after.

Third Party or No?

So where should conservatives put their time and energy?

How do you vote when the third party candidate agrees with the GOP platform and the Republican candidate doesn't? Isn't it best to encourage the candidate who *does* agree with such a common sense conservative document?

That's where it's best for our cause to vote third party. It makes our votes quantifiable and qualitatively obvious – the Establishment and the candidates, win or lose, know why people were so upset with them they couldn't be convinced to vote their way.

If they want those votes back they'll need to change their views and/or behavior in future elections.

I've heard many suggest (more training from the Establishment) that third party voting "to send a signal" is okay in districts where the race isn't close.

That's getting it backward.

It registers on the "mind" of a major party if their candidate wins by only 200 votes and a third party candidate took 700 votes in that same district.

It registers *even more* if that major party candidate *lost* by only 200 votes!

So to properly influence major parties, close districts aren't where you want to *avoid* making an impact, for fear of causing the "lesser of two evils" candidate to lose.

Those districts are where it's *most important* to make an impact, because it costs the major parties more to ignore you.

It provides an incentive for the major party and its candidates to modify their behavior and adopt those positions which will be most attractive to potential third party voters.

For this to work, conservative and liberty minded voters *must* vote third party if the major party candidate is not sufficiently on target.

The corollary is that such voters *must* vote for the *major party candidate* when that candidate *does* adhere to your principles.

Failure to do so in those cases is where your vote really *does* create a negative spoiler effect which benefits neither you nor those candidates who agree with you.

I believe "party first" thinking is detrimental to principle even if your party is a third party.

You're continuing to punish them for past wrongs even when they try to correct it, which is a violation of the principle of intentional voting.

Vote for ideas and ideals (and character), not party!

Victory in 2014

If Republicans win in 2014 – if the "wave" happens, as I certainly think it should, intentional voting or no – they need to take leadership. How, with Obama still in the White House?

We need to be a brick wall to stop anything Obama and the Democrats try to do. We *have* to do that – that's the reason behind why millions of Americans are voting GOP in the first place.

But we can't be *just* that. The Democrats in power today have shown themselves very good at placing blame, and having it stick. We need to do some of that ourselves.

People will quibble as to how effective Gingrich was, in the wake of the 1994 wave election and his taking over as Speaker. But few will doubt that he showed extraordinary leadership and pluck as an opposition leader in the years leading up to 1994. He gave President Clinton hell, stymied everything he wanted to do, and made the American people realize he was protecting the country from bad policy.

By contrast with the recent government shutdowns, Gingrich's shutdown was pretty successful, and was a public relations coup. People realized they didn't really notice that the federal government was shut down, and they didn't mind it so much. He proved a point.

But I'm not talking about shutdowns either. Such tactics are necessary to stop a reckless overgrowth of the budget, which has increased at a breakneck pace since just before Obama took office. But the GOP can't be "the party of 'no.'"

To set things up for 2016, Republicans need to take leadership of the agenda. Obama, helpfully, has already practically vacated the office. He's on the golf course during major crises because he knows he has no idea how to fix things, and he doesn't care. He already has one foot out the door. This will be all the more apparent if the GOP leadership starts actually stepping up, and if they take the opportunity to demonstrate the supremacy of conservative ideas and policies.

We need to propose *real* solutions to America's problems, and start passing things through both houses of Congress to dispel the "do-nothing Congress" stigma. If Republicans in both houses are able to craft bipartisan legislation, taking advantage of issue-cleavages within the Democrat Party, and send it to the President's desk, he'll have to find some excuse not to do anything with them.

Out of power, the Democrats in Congress will have lost the ability to put coalitions together behind dangerous or progressive legislation.

That is, *unless the RINOs get re-elected!*

If conservatives are running the show in 2015, and not the Establishment, we have a sterling opportunity to show how powerless the Democrats are to solve America's problems, and demonstrate to America how there's another way to overcome our problems.

A way they can vote for in 2016.

Conservatives don't necessarily have to win all the offices up in 2014. They have to win enough to tip the balance of control within the party. To bolster the ranks and give the real Constitutionalists and Reagan Republicans the courage to stand up and put new leadership in place of the failed Boehner and McConnell. Or, somehow, maybe force those two to dance to a conservative tune – McConnell, at least, used to be considered one of us.

The Shining City on a Hill

Only true conservatives, constitutionalists and liberty activists are going to be able to rescue America from the morass it's gotten itself into.

Fresh ideas. True ideals. Renewed promise.

We have to have enough confidence in our vision to communicate it to new generations – to educate and raise up new, young conservatives who understand why principles mean something and how principled policy formulations can rescue America and make it what it was meant to be.

Teach them how to use *principle*, not government, to make our country a better place.

We have to recruit and train a new generation of conservative candidates to take on the Establishment candidates, and the backstabbers who've chosen a new Establishment master.

This new generation of conservative candidates will need to know how to get out front, to define their ideas and themselves to the public before their opponents do it for them.

And we have to be willing to support these candidates, with volunteer hours and financial donations.

Not through the Party – *never* through the Party! – but to candidates directly, or through committees pledged to support only platform-abiding candidates.

We have to enable these candidates to succeed. It's harder and harder today for candidates to succeed through merely passion and the sweat of their brow, and those of their volunteers.

But we can do it!

We can take our country back.

Imagine America resonating, once more to a conservative message, inspirational, articulately described and passionately presented!

Remember how you felt when Ronald Reagan was president.

A shining city on a hill. We can have that, again.

We have to be willing to use our votes intentionally, to maintain quality control and to band together with other like minded people who are just as frustrated.

Let's make this happen.

Afterword

I feel like this book has such a potential to change things for the better in the conservative movement.

If you agree, and I hope you do, *I need your help!*

I'm just one guy – I can't spread the word of this book, or its important message as far as our team can. That's you!

Will you please help me?

Tell your friends about this on social media. Recommend it to them in person. If you wouldn't mind buying extra copies (paperback is easier for this, for obvious reasons) and gifting them to people who you think would be receptive or people who need to see it (whether they're on our side or not), that will spread the message.

We're on the verge of a revolution here – a needed, positive change in paradigm and direction.

Anything you can do to help contributes to the cause.

We can't be tentative or hesitant about this. If you talk to five people about it, and only one listens, that's progress. It's that 20 percent of us who will change things. Twenty percent, or even ten, of any population can achieve dramatic things.

Especially on the margins, which is where we have the ability to succeed. That margin becomes exponentially more powerful when using the tactics of intentional voting and pressure politics.

In order to keep up on events and news, I'd again invite you to please "like" my author page on Facebook (Facebook.com/conservativechange), follow me on Twitter (@ReagansLegacy), and sign up for my e-newsletter through my

Blog, at LookOnTheRightSide.com. I should always be reachable at edhanks.com.

Lastly, please don't forget there is a preview of my upcoming Personhood book right after this. I hope you will support the Personhood movement, and follow the news about Personhood through the Persons Not Property Facebook group and/or my e-newsletter as listed on my blog (Lookontherightside.com). If I have sufficient funds at my disposal to start an organization to promote Personhood, it will be hosted at personsnotproperty.org (which should for now forward to a page promoting this book).

Note to Readers:

I'm aware that many of you may have ordered this book shortly before, or even shortly after, the 2014 November elections, and some parts of the conclusion to this book refer to that election in the future tense.

It's my intent to publish a 2nd Edition shortly after the 2014 General Election, offering analysis of the results, and making sure my book squares with what we saw that November.

Before I publish a 2nd Edition, I will post most or all of the review and significant changes in a blog post at LookOnTheRightSide.com. So you can easily find anything you might have missed there.

You're also welcome to contact me at coloconservative@gmail.com to request a link or the full text of the blog post by e-mail.

Preview:
An Introduction to Pro-Life
Personhood

There is a new trend in pro-life politics.

After 30 or 40 years many pro-lifers looked back and saw little practical progress from the traditional anti-abortion strategy of "chipping away" at Roe v. Wade through regulations. They could identify even *less* ground gained in terms of a cultural paradigm shift. The public might express personal opposition to abortion, but still followed the narrative of "a right to choose."

Sometime between 2004 and 2006 these frustrated pro-lifers banded together and decided to change the game.

They turned, instead, to the concept of Human Personhood – treating every human being as deserving of a Right to Life which should be protected by the government.

No more splitting the difference. No more forcing people to jump through hoops in order to make abortion more difficult in hopes they would make a different "choice" and not kill their child.

The new movement understood that we needed to teach society to accept a paradigm shift. Abortion is *always* wrong because murder of an innocent unborn child is a crime against humanity, no matter the circumstances.

There's not supposed to be any "choice" with regard to murder.

But Roe v. Wade, in 1973, ruled an unborn child is not a legal person and is therefore the mother's property. She can "choose" what to do with "it" (not him or her).

The "chipping away" strategy has always played on that turf – "Yes, it's a choice, but let's put hedges on that choice to mitigate the harm."

By contrast, the Personhood movement has left behind the Roe v. Wade model of an unborn child as the property of the mother – the philosophical "playing ground" of the pro-abortion side – and turned instead to treatment of the unborn child as a human being with fundamental human rights.

Back when both the pro-life and pro-abortion sides' strategies more or less agreed that the unborn child was the mother's property, it was easy to say "you have to meet these criteria before you're allowed to abort your child."

That was the *practical* method of reducing the number of abortions.

But that approach logically denied the Personhood of the unborn child. As the U.S. Supreme Court *correctly* recognized in its Roe v. Wade decision, if an unborn child *were* a Person under the law – if he or she were human beings – then it would be automatically illegal to kill them under any circumstances without due process of law.

Being Trained

Personhood had always been the ideal – the ultimate goal. But it was seen by many as an impossible dream after Roe v. Wade.

To go back to the primary theme of *How To Train Your Politician*, rank and file pro-lifers didn't intentionally or even consciously accept the "child as property" model in place of the Personhood model after Roe v. Wade.

Some of the leadership did. Not all. They gave up and gave in on total victory, at least for the foreseeable future.

An Establishment regime grew within the pro-life community, same as in the Republican Party. And this Establishment pro-life leadership – led first and foremost by National Right to Life and Americans United for Life – intentionally embraced compromise after concluding abortion was a permanent fact of life and would never be abolished.

They set their goal as reducing the number of abortions through regulatory laws, believing anything more ambitious was bound to fail.

Given that assumption, their reaction made sense on a practical level, if not in terms of moral principles.

I want to emphasize that we shouldn't despise leaders for doing what they were convinced was best, even if they rejected good advice from those who counseled against compromise. We have a lot of people in this movement who've put their hearts and souls and fortunes into the pro-life cause, and believed they were doing good all the while. Politics gets into any movement, and we can disagree, but we should not forget our intent and our goals are ultimately the same.

I can fault leaders for their mistakes and missteps without condemning them. I honor pro-lifers for the contributions they believed they were making.

But these nationally influential pro-life groups – the Establishment – began to train pro-life activists and voters to accept compromise as a way of getting things done. Just as the GOP Establishment trained conservatives to think things that weren't true and to vote in ways that undermined their own interests, National Right to Life and Americans United for Life trained candidates, officials and voters to work for compromise *as if it would someday end abortion* (though logically that could never happen through compromise).

Again, I don't mean to suggest nefarious motives. They faced the same dilemma Christian voters do, and they chose to follow a path they perceived as the lesser of two evils.

But they also engaged in an incestuous relationship with the GOP Establishment. The Pro-Life Establishment trained its voters to support pro-choice Establishment Republicans while the GOP Establishment encouraged its candidates and officials to talk big about abortion at election time while doing very little on a practical level to end or even limit the practice of abortion.

In return, national pro-life groups got access in Washington D.C. and the GOP Establishment gained acceptance into pro-life circles.

The new status quo began to feel comfortable.

Now, many pro-lifers feel it's been too comfortable for too many decades.

It's time to shake things up.

A Return to Principle

Some large but less influential groups – American Life League and Human Life International leap to mind – maintained that we had to hold on to principle. They avoided compromise and steadfastly fought to restore recognition of the humanity of the unborn and to end abortion from conception on, no exceptions. They always held to the Personhood strategy, even through decades when it was deemed unrealistic by other pro-lifers.

It's taken nearly 40 years, but eventually the pro-life movement – most of it – has returned to the Personhood principle.

Since 2006 Personhood has caught on like wildfire and has earned a controversial reputation.

On the one hand the strategy has made impressive inroads into both the pro-life community as a whole, and into the broader political community. In 2012, five of the six top contenders for the Republican nomination for president pledged to support the Personhood principle (Romney being the lone holdout).

Personhood has also earned a nasty reputation among *some* Republicans as an "election killer" – a third rail that most politicians shouldn't dare touch, lest it make them easy targets and they go down in flames in November.

The main reason why that has happened is messaging, both pro and con.

Democrats and pro-abortion groups claimed Personhood would ban in-vitro fertilization, some "common forms of birth control," and could require investigations of women who have miscarriages. Most of these claims were ludicrous – obviously false, once you understand what a Personhood law actually does. And the issues with IVF and birth control were presented in wildly misleading ways. But they were made, nonetheless, embraced by the media, and believed by many members of the public, including some pro-life conservatives who should know better.

Strict Catholics hold that birth control of any form, other than "natural family planning," is a rejection of God's will, and also rejects the value of a child, treating children as "unwanted" rather than as blessings. Naturally if someone uses birth control and it fails – they still get pregnant – the child seems an imposition for that family, or a "problem," which is often "solved" by recourse to abortion or abortifacients (even by Christians). Some Protestants are coming to agree with this position, and may begin to advocate against birth control in general, but this argument is *entirely* separate from the Personhood debate.

Republican candidates were untrained in how to respond when accused of "opposing access to contraceptives" (which Personhood does *not* affect). Regardless, the easy answer to charges is Personhood can't affect any product or practice which cannot kill an already conceived human child – a legitimate human individual with his or her own unique DNA.

Messaging is also necessary to allow the general public to understand what Personhood *really* is, as opposed to how it's been framed by Democrats and the media.

Personhood has become the Democrats' new "easy button."

Since they have no regard for the truth, they've gotten into the habit of running ads against *every* Republican, charging they're for "banning" birth control.

The media has been unhelpful in uncovering the truth about Personhood. Since the media greatly influences public opinion, the public is afraid of Personhood. It's been incorrectly branded, and people have responded by avoiding the Personhood candidates.

Again, that's an education issue. The Reaganesque solution is this. Learn why Personhood is not extreme, how it is, in fact, perfectly mainstream and rational. Then explain to the media, and to the public, why they should support Personhood too.

Then Personhood could become an electoral advantage rather than a liability. It's already an advantage in many districts and states.

The message is already getting out. It helped that the furor over Hobby Lobby's lawsuit brought these same issues of abortifacients vs. "contraceptives" into the light.

One ironic result of this publicity – one that could end up *undermining* its value for Democrats – is that it allows a more public, more widespread discussion of what "birth control" really is, as opposed to "contraceptives."

More and more people among the general population are starting to realize that *some forms of "birth control" may actually kill their own children before they even know they're pregnant.*

The Slavery Issue of Our Day

The Republican Party today, as with slavery a century and a half ago, has the opportunity to stand on another major, unifying principle which could inspire them to victory. They could pledge to ban abortion as a violation of fundamental human rights and recognize the Personhood of the unborn child so he or she is not considered property like the slaves.

Counting deaths by surgical abortion alone, the United States has seen 50-70 million unborn children slaughtered since the first laws legalizing abortion in 1967. Its ramifications for the country are earthshattering.

212

This is the "slavery issue" of the 21st Century, just as the evil of slavery was the defining issue of the early- to mid-1800s.

Politicians may claim other issues are far more important. But this is the most important issue we face in this country – whether the slaughter will continue, or whether our country has the moral courage to put an end to the yearly execution of 1.6 million unborn children (at least a million more per year if you count chemical abortions).

History shows vast numbers of Americans voted primarily on the issue of slavery – the moral issue that was eating away at the heart of this country back then.

It's my opinion that the Republican Party will succeed or die on this principle in coming years.

Any attempts to remove the pro-life principle from the platform will destroy the party so that a half-century from today the Republican Party will be as well known as the Whigs are today.

I believe Personhood will be recognized as a human rights principle with or without the GOP being on board.

It will happen with or without the GOP. History marches forward.

It's worth noting that abortion is also the Democrats' "slavery issue," every bit as much as the Republicans'.

For Republicans, or potentially for a third party if Republicans abdicate their responsibility, abortion is an opportunity to dominate politics once public opinion is transformed in favor of justice for the unborn. But, today and in the future, abortion no longer works as a net benefit wedge issue for Democrats – the significance of "standing for a woman's right to choose" has been lessening year by year as public opinion has shifted against abortion.

That's why Democrats have stopped defending "abortion" in ads, and now talk mostly about "birth control."

In fact, abortion has now become a wedge issue that favors Republicans, and a drag upon Democrat prospects – a liability.

Democrats still feel beholden to the abortion lobby because many Democrat activists and officeholders have been trained to knee-jerk support of abortion "rights."

And, perhaps more importantly, the abortion lobby provides volumes of funding for Democrat candidates.

But at some point that money will not be able to compensate for the liability of voter revulsion at blanket Democrat support for abortion through 9 months of pregnancy.

Personhood Is Gaining Ground, Not Losing

How realistic is the chance of Personhood's passing, somewhere, and thereby becoming an issue that could reach the Supreme Court and challenging Roe v. Wade?

The strategy has been pooh-poohed by opponents, within and outside of the pro-life community.

They often cite two things: 1) Personhood Amendments failed twice in Colorado, maxing out at only 30% support (news reports often say it was defeated by a vote of 3:1, which if you do the math is clearly false), and 2) a Personhood Amendment was narrowly rejected even in Mississippi, which has been called the "most pro-life state."

Mockers say, "If it can't pass in Mississippi, it won't pass *anywhere!*"

Such criticisms miss some of the main dynamics.

For one, Personhood is a process of education. It's a new paradigm for the public. And it's fighting uphill against powerful lies and misrepresentations.

Nevertheless, it is succeeding, gradually. Step by step.

Polls in 2008 showed that only about 12% of Americans would have supported a complete ban on abortion. But even in "purple state" Colorado we've found as many as 1 in 3 voters ready to ban abortion outright, including abortifacient birth control.

That's progress!

Personhood has had a significant hearing in at least 12 states since 2008, through either proposed amendments or considered legislation.

Petitioners in California collected more than a million signatures from citizens there.

Colorado has Personhood on the ballot again in 2014. This measure is not strictly an "abortion ban" amendment. Instead it is a non-compromised, Personhood-compliant incremental fetal homicide regulation (i.e. without the drawbacks of regulations that treat unborn children as property) to protect the rights of unborn children in criminal cases such as vehicular homicide.

Personhood legislation – in the form of a Human Life Amendment, or Life at Conception legislation – has been on the table in the US Congress for many years. It's become more popular in recent years. Recent versions in the US Senate have had as many as 15 cosponsors, including "big names" like Lamar Alexander, Roy Blunt, John Boozman, Dan Coats, Tom Coburn, Michael Enzi, James Inhofe, Mike Johanns, Rand Paul, John Thune and David Vitter. Similar legislation in the US House has scores of cosponsors.

Political support for Personhood will only increase as pro-life groups and pro-life voters adopt Personhood standards, as candidates learn about and adopt these positions, and as voters become familiar with Personhood and apply it as a gateway issue in the voting booth.

Now, a caution. For the first time in decades, the Gallup Poll recently showed fewer people self-identify as pro-life. Some in the anti-abortion movement have been discouraged by this. I am not.

If someone tries to tell you this is a sign Personhood is hurting the movement, don't believe them!

It is my hypothesis that this is not because fewer people oppose abortion, or have softened their opinions against surgical abortion. Instead, I believe the definition of "pro-life" has changed in the minds of the public. After campaigns for Personhood in a dozen states, plus the widespread exposure via conservative media to the discussion about abortifacient birth control related to the Hobby Lobby refusal to pay for only those four specific types of birth control, it is my opinion that a new bar has been set for the definition of "pro-life."

Those who tell Gallup they're "pro-life" are, I believe, increasingly not just against surgical abortion, but against abortifacient birth control as well. Whereas the reduction in self-identified pro-lifers could be a reflection of those who continue to be against surgical abortion, but who don't yet understand the equivalency of chemical abortions. Someone who believe the progressive narrative and now thinks "pro-life" means "opposed to birth control" will naturally self-identify as "pro-choice" when polled, whereas they might not have before the Personhood and Hobby Lobby things came up.

So, in light of this new discussion, we've seen a new "exception" crop up – support for abortifacient birth control. Some Republican candidates, including prominent US Senate candidates in 2014, have taken this a step further by endorsing "over-the-counter" birth control, which unless specifically excepted must mean abortifacients. Rep. Cory Gardner (R-CO), for instance, renounced Personhood at about the same time he embraced the over-the-counter birth control argument. We've already demonstrated that Personhood doesn't have any impact upon contraceptives – only against abortifacients – so by process of elimination we can only assume he intends abortifacients to be offered over-the-counter.

I should also mention that Personhood has caught fire even outside of the United States, in places like the Dominican Republic, Chile, Costa Rica and Poland, among others. The Vatican has aided in bringing the Personhood debate to the European Union. It is getting a surprisingly fair hearing at the

United Nations. The nation of Bulgaria even re-wrote their Constitution to include Personhood protections for unborn children.

Is Personhood A Wise Strategy?

Not all critics of Personhood are pro-abortion. Some are sincere pro-lifers who are stuck in the old paradigm. Many of them are convinced Personhood won't work, or could make things worse.

Clarke Forsythe is senior counsel for Americans United for Life – one of the groups that prefers a regulatory framework to limit abortion, and which so far has strongly opposed Personhood as a strategy. In one of Forsythe's books, he charges, "Until Roe is overturned, such [Personhood] bills have no chance of going into effect and being enforced. If introduced by a single legislator, they will not be considered by a committee and will never come to a vote."

His predictions on legislative action have already been proved not true. There have been several true Personhood bills in several states that have been heard in committee, some actually passing through the committee to the floor of the House or Senate, some even passing by majority vote through one chamber, and some even having support from the Governor (though in those cases it didn't make it all the way to his desk).

Forsythe also conveniently ignores legal points that show a Personhood argument benefits from the very text of Roe v. Wade. In the Supreme Court's own words, "If this [the State of Texas'] suggestion of personhood is established, the appellant's [pro-abortion] case collapses, for the fetus' right to life is then guaranteed by the 14th Amendment."

The 14th Amendment is like King Kong to Roe v. Wade's chimpanzee – if Personhood triggers the 14th Amendment's equal protection clause, Roe v. Wade doesn't even stand a chance in a pure legal sense.

Granted, there is no guarantee the Supreme Court will use logic or fairness, or even the rule of law, to make their determination.

Earlier I pointed out that no justice on the current Supreme Court believes in a Right to Life for the unborn.

Pro-life opponents of the Personhood strategy point to a memo by National Right to Life attorney James Bopp, which claims they fear a challenge to Roe v. Wade now might "make things worse." But they're speaking out of both sides of their mouth. National Right to Life is itself seeking to pass regulatory measures in many states which they "hope" will go to the Supreme Court!

So if they don't want abortion to go to the Supreme Court... Hmm...

Plus, how could things possibly get worse? Over 1 million children will die from abortion this year!

If this Court refuses to acknowledge the Personhood of the unborn, we need to begin right away (like, now! – don't wait to see) in replacing them with justices who do.

Understand that the Supreme Court does not always have the final word. Technically the 1858 Dred Scott decision was never overturned by the Court. Congress, instead, added amendments to the Constitution to instruct the Supreme Court about what the new law was. "New law" is the role of Congress, not the Court. Congress changed the rules by which the Court could judge future cases.

"Party first" fans will pooh-pooh. Congress and the states, they will say, would never get to the point where they'd approve a constitutional amendment to that effect. "You will never reach that degree of unanimity on subjects as controversial as abortion."

Oh? Ten years after the Voting Rights Act, how many members of Congress were opposed to the voting rights of Blacks? How large was their faction? How many would vote to put Blacks back in the back of the bus?

Once the public mind changes – fundamentally – on an issue, the politicians will never look back. Those who refuse to compromise lose their offices. Those who know what's best for them adopt the position held by the public.

Remember the anti-slavery movement. Remember the American civil rights movement.

It's possible to change the world. In a relatively short period of time.

The answer to the question - Is Personhood a Wise Strategy? - is this: Personhood is the *only* strategy that will get rid of abortion forever, and protect the rest of the human person too, in an age of cloning and euthanasia and genetic manipulation and astonishing advances in science that outstrip advances in the study of human ethics.

Every argument against Personhood, either from pro-aborts or from pro-life critics, can be solidly refuted, which I will do when I publish my Personhood book (sometime in 2015, I expect).

Anti-Abortion Regulations Hurt the Cause

I meet many pro-lifers who support both, Personhood and anti-abortion regulations.

I appreciate their stand. They are eternal optimists, just as I normally am. Their heart is definitely in the right place. But I must offer a caution.

I hate to bring this up because it is such an emotional issue. Many of us have invested portions of our lives and fortunes for the cause, and many people have done so on behalf of anti-abortion regulations, hoping they would improve things.

It is my contention that regulations do not have the ability to turn public opinion against abortion.

I also contend it does the pro-life movement no long-term good to pass these regulatory laws.

I even go so far as to suggest anti-abortion regulations hurt the cause, by essentially arguing against the principle of a Right to Life. There is legal advice which I will detail in the Personhood book which suggests these efforts can actually undermine the legal status of the unborn in law! End note 54 of the Roe v. Wade decision suggests as much.

There is a caveat to all this. Anti-abortion regulations are unhelpful because they treat the unborn child as property, and many or most of them actually write into statute when abortion is legal – a tricky situation where pro-life legislators actually end up authorizing abortion under certain conditions with their own legislation.

But it's possible to do almost any type of anti-abortion legislation in a life-affirming, "Personhood compliant" way. It has to do with how you write the laws. For instance the Personhood compliant fetal homicide amendment on the 2014 ballot in Colorado is "incremental" in nature – it doesn't outlaw abortion. It applies only when a prosecutable crime is committed which takes the life of an unborn child. It affirms life in that way, and does not treat the unborn child in any circumstance as property – it would have these children protected as persons under the law. Nothing in the language of the amendment suggests that any unborn child is not a person – it simply limits its scope to prosecutable crimes such as vehicular homicide or assault.

It's certainly possible to impose regulations on abortion clinics (as "medical facilities") through Personhood-compliant legislation, or even ultrasound or parental notification legislation. It depends how they're written.

What cannot be Personhood compliant is something like a "Heartbeat bill," which may affirm the lives of humans past the 20-week threshold, but which suggest that unborn children younger than that are not worthy of protection. It promotes a false definition of humanity based on how old you are, or which biological functions you have, which is not life affirming at all. These proposed laws are still playing on the same "Roe v. Wade field" which assumes a human being starts as subhuman property and becomes "emancipated" at some point. The Heartbeat bill says 20 weeks, or 15. But it might as well be birth – it's drawing the same line dividing humanity from pre-humanity, just setting it at a different place, as if it were government's job to decide which humans are really people or not.

It rejects and speaks against the concept of a Right to Life for all human beings, of a value based not on a person's capabilities or status in life, like a utilitarian or caste system, but on their mere humanity.

At the very least, I strenuously argue that traditionally written anti-abortion regulations are a waste of time, and 100 percent of our pro-life resources should be directed toward spreading the transformative message of Personhood to the general public. We can change public opinion, but only if we make a concerted effort. We've been failing at that for 40 years. Let's switch things up!

Again, if you have a strategy that's not working – that may achieve "something," but isn't getting you closer to your ultimate goal – it's time to change strategies.

The immediate response of sincere pro-lifers is usually, "But we have to save the babies we can now, and eventually we'll save them all."

This thinking is wrongheaded – part of our Establishment pro-life training.

If you had to choose, which of the following seems like it saves more babies?

1) Spending 10 years saving 20,000 babies per year with regulations, then after 10 years turning to the Personhood strategy to finally abolish abortion forever.

2) Spending four or six years actively trying to change society's mind about abortion by arguing for the humanity of the unborn and protection of their human rights through Personhood.

Remember, there are more than 1 million babies dying from abortion each year. Using the model above, even though it seems like "progress" to save 20,000 babies per year, the regulation path still allows more than a million abortions to continue every year until abolition is finally achieved (totaling 200,000 saved babies vs. 10 million dead babies).

By doing the math you'll see the "immediatist" Personhood path – the complete abolition of abortion – even if it takes six years to accomplish, still saves at least 5 million more babies than the regulation strategy over that 10 year period.

And then it's over – no more slaughter.

Anti-abortion regulations are small potatoes. Even the more effective regulations aren't going to save more than a tenth of those babies otherwise scheduled for death each year.

Anti-abortion regulators have a "20-year plan" to end abortion gradually.

Personhood and the associated Abolish Human Abortion (AHA) movement has a 5-10 year plan to get rid of legal abortion utterly.

It is a far more ambitious and forward looking strategy.

Even regulators say they'll turn to Personhood "when the time is right."

The time is now!

Think back to the subchapter on Inspiration. *Leaders* don't wait for public opinion to change. They *lead* it. They make history by shaping the world around them.

That's us. Let's do it!

Non-Personhood Candidates Are Obstacles

Now, on to another upsetting, emotional subject.

Some legislators who have made their names by pushing compromise legislation may feel bound to defend their record, and so may remain entrenched in the regulatory mentality despite good reasons to support Personhood.

However, in my experience, most of these legislators are willing to endorse Personhood. I consider them to be "on our side" even if they don't renounce regulations.

There's something else we have to be watchful for, though. Something that could stymie our every effort to abolish abortion.

Due to the same dynamics described in the early chapters of this book, legislators or candidates for executive office (governors, presidents) who don't hold to a Personhood standard will be obstacles.

They could prevent us from protecting the unborn, no matter what party they belong to.

Those candidates who are not fully pro-life will, once in office, actually oppose any legislation that supports the Right to Life. Why? Because establishing a Right to Life would make those exceptions they believe in illegal.

The fact is, politicians who are "pro-life with exceptions" are in favor of at least some child killing as government policy. "But only a few – not a lot!"

Unfortunately, we've seen this in practice.

President George W. Bush ran on a pro-life platform, and most pro-lifers supported him because they believed he was as pro-life as they were. But when Bush was faced with a principled choice in South Dakota in 2006 – a total ban on abortion – which side did he choose? He exerted pressure against the initiative effort, which ultimately failed by only a few percentage points (and might have succeeded had he supported it instead of opposed it).

His position was that it must have exceptions for rape and incest or he would oppose it.

President Bush – our "pro-life" president – basically vetoed a total ban on abortion because it didn't allow the relatively small number of abortions he supported (about 8,000 babies' lives per year).

Bush was also the first president to provide public funding for experiments upon, and destruction of, embryos in "existing lines." It was part of his "ban" on embryonic stem cell research that most people never realized had a sinister caveat.

Likewise, as we go forward we can expect non-Personhood politicians *from either party* to be the ones who will oppose our efforts to protect all unborn children.

Moreover, any judges these politicians put forward will be of the same mind until we insist that they must approve only pro-Personhood judges.

Without holding the line on Personhood as a gateway standard, we'll never get enough favorable justices to protect unborn childrens' human rights.

We need to end this era of compromise, when even our "pro-life" officeholders support some forms of abortion. We will face this problem with all candidates until we insist that they be supportive of an actual Right to Life guaranteed by government and Constitution (as it says it should be).

Training Pro-Life Candidates

Once upon a time, it was typical to ask a candidate first, "Are you pro-life?" Then, "Where are you on the 'exceptions?'" Basically, under which circumstances would you allow the baby to be killed? Rape? Incest? To save the life of the mother? The health of the mother? Or they would only oppose "partial-birth abortions?" Or even that?

For decades, the Republican Party actively pushed for rape and incest exceptions which undermine the Right to Life. Why? Because they wanted to more easily elect Republicans, and it was easier to not have to explain why abortion is wrong even in cases of rape or incest.

Even solidly pro-life candidates, whose conscience told them not to compromise, were instructed by the Party to embrace exceptions for the "hard cases" or they would never find any support.

Today this is changing. It is critically important that we hold candidates to oppose all abortion, therefore we need to make sure we pin down their real position and get assurances.

Given the chance, any Republican politician is going to call him or herself "pro-life" – they'll define it however they want, and may mean the opposite of what you mean. They'll do it to benefit themselves.

One candidate for Congress said he was "100% pro-life" and believed "life begins at conception." But, when pressed, it turned out he didn't believe it was the government's responsibility to pass or enforce laws against abortion, so he was essentially "0% pro-life" and was just lying to get pro-life votes.

If the first words of response to the question "are you pro-life" are "I'm opposed to federal funding of abortions" it's a good sign they're not really that pro-life. Otherwise, they would have mentioned some stronger position. All Libertarians, so far as I know, are opposed to federal funding for abortions, but most of them are officially pro-choice.

Therefore, pro-life constituencies and groups must maintain solid accountability measures to weed out the fakers from the real pro-lifers. The main concern is that politicians must promise to support no abortions, and must also promise to support Personhood legislation if it comes before them.

Plain and simple, Personhood for the unborn is the definition of pro-life. Period. Otherwise, we're forced to settle for politicians who would "only kill a few children."

Can It Really Be Done?

Maybe you think passing Personhood – abolishing abortion – is too much to hope for, even over the course of six years.

Maybe you think it'll take ten years. Or twenty.

Do the math over however many years you think it'll take. If you're saving 20,000 babies a year through regulations, or even a very unrealistic 100,000 babies a year, you're still better off working to pass Personhood, and will save more babies over the long run.

Personhood shuts down 100% of legal abortions, every year from the time it's first passed! That's a million babies a year, saved. At least!

The case for Personhood has already affected the public mind significantly, after attempts to pass Personhood Amendments in a dozen states, and after the very public Hobby Lobby case.

You can spend the next several years beating your head against a wall, trying to change the public mind with regulations, but each year you don't turn to the Personhood strategy is another year we're not making the case to society that unborn children are human beings, deserving of an actual, inviolable, Right to Life.

Because they tacitly accept the view of unborn children as property, not as persons, anti-abortion regulations may stop some abortions, but they actually make abortion more popular provided it's hemmed in with "appropriate regulations to stop abuses."

That's exactly what William Wilberforce noticed with regard to the British anti-slavery efforts, and you can see those same attitudes mirrored in the United States as anti-slavery regulations were passed to prevent abuses of peoples' "property" (similar to present-day laws protecting animals from abuse by their owners). The "protections" in the law – the anti-slavery regulations – were seen as *improving* the institution of slavery, such that it was less abusive and more a positive thing when handled properly.

Personhood is a paradigm shift for the public, and it's one we have to argue for. But we're better off arguing for it, rather than essentially arguing against the humanity of the unborn child by wasting our time confusing the public mind by protecting babies with regulations that are akin to animal cruelty statutes.

Millions of babies are dying every year we don't abolish abortion.

It's inhumane. It's inhuman. It's worse than slavery. It's a stain upon our souls and our honor as a nation.

God has clearly blessed America. But how can He bless us today while this goes on?

As with slavery, it is up to us – those who bear His name – to summon the courage to end it.

Notes on the Book:

Notes on the Book:

Notes on the Book: